THE LOOP OF TRANSFORMATION

PAUL DOUGLAS CASTLE

BLUEPRINT PRESS
INTERNATIONALE

ISBN
978-1-961117-65-5 (Paperback)
978-1-961117-66-2 (eBook)
978-1-961117-78-5 (Hardcover)

Dedications

Precious and wonderful is our loving Most High God, and I thank Him for the prophets, disciples, and Yeshua. The awesome Bible is His inspired and glorious works of righteousness, and I am certain He wrote it to increase great understanding of His ways.

Beyond the shadow of a doubt, our eternal life in the heavens above or on this Earth depends on us knowing Him and walking in His ways. Please realize it's the perfect word of God, the prophets and the Son of God teach, giving us the ability to know our great Creator well. Their lives became entwined with His gospel, and they had no other interests.

Therefore, when we stand before God's throne someday, we give an account of ourselves; then it'll be better for us if we know much about God. If we are Bible-savvy and understand His word, We can say we had an extremely special relationship with Him while we were alive.

Indeed, when we stand before God someday, and it's our turn to give an account of ourselves, it would satisfy our souls to know we dedicated enough time to learn about Him while living on this Earth.

Positively, I dedicate this book first to my wonderful God and His righteous ways. Also, I dedicate this book to Paul Castle II, Kathy Sue Hager, and my grandson Bryan Paul Castle, especially to Bryan, for inspiring me to forgo foolishness and replace it with righteousness.

TABLE OF CONTENTS

ACKNOWLEDGMENTS

In all the following stories, wherever scriptures appear, they are taken from the King James Special Study Edition Bible. The Special Study Edition Bible, excellent and valuable to all of mankind, is a road map to the kingdom of God. The Global Bible Society published it.

I sincerely thank the Global Bible Society for their wonderful work with their God-inspired Special Study Edition Bible. I want you to know that everything else written in this book is my analogy, and my analogy is based on the wonderful word of God as I understand it.

God bless you
Sincerely, Paul Douglas Castle
Bible story writer
Theologian of the heart
Creative story designer

CHAPTER ONE

THE LOOP OF TRANSFORMATION

This informative story, bold and revealing, is *The Loop Of Transformation*. It looks into the future and to a prophesized time, paralleling the Abomination of Desolation. I want you to know when the Loop Of Transformation forms, Lucifer will be standing on this Earth in his physical form.

This story, we need to understand, reveals a redesigning of the population on the surface of this Earth and exposes what happens to the angelic and spirit prisoners after the gates of Hell are opened, after thousands of years of incarceration.

However, please remember our body formations change after we die, and there are no flesh and blood bodies locked away in the pits of Hell. But only the spirits of ungodly people and the indestructible physical bodies of the rebellious angels who are exiled and locked away in the pits of Hell.

During the first four thousand years after the flood, the wicked Lucifer and his evil army of rebellious angels are imprisoned in Hell. Indeed, they've had a lot of time to plan what they'll do when released from the pits of Hell.

I assure you, just because they are evil and rebellious angels locked away in the pits of Hell, it doesn't mean they aren't highly intelligent. I want you to know they are desperate to come back to the surface of this Earth and be as they were before the flood, and be aware they are extremely resourceful and desperate rebellious angels.

Most people are blind to what they cannot see and do not consider what's happening within the pits of Hell. But deep within the Earth's center, where the hot lava flows, it could be the location of the most sophisticated workshop in the universe, and there isn't any reason to believe differently.

During the last four thousand years of incarceration in Hell, I assure you, the wicked, rebellious angels, locked away from the beautiful surface of the Earth. They've been busy angels, not sitting around in rocking chairs or idle by the fire.

Indeed, they've had plenty of time to reshape and transform themselves into fierce fighting creatures ready for war. This analogy means they've been readying themselves for the coming day when they'll be released onto the Earth among us frailer creations.

I want you to realize that the rebellious angels aren't dumb angels, and they haven't been sitting in Hell on a homemade chair and idling the day away because they need to survive or be killed. I believe they've been planning for the coming battle; they anticipate fighting with the wonderful Son of God for planet Earth.

However, I want you to know reshaping themselves into fierce fighting machines means they'll look monstrous compared to anything we can imagine. I believe the monstrous Frankenstein's descriptions of themselves are made from their own D.N.A.

Indeed, these hideous, out-of-this-world Frankenstein descriptions of themselves aren't symbolic descriptions of manmade machines, as many preachers assume about them. However, everything that ascends to the surface of this Earth will be a transformation of the literal.

I assure you, during the seven years, or the last forty-two months of the great tribulation time, coming soon upon this Earth. There will be out-of-this-world creations on this Earth that will be different from anything mankind has ever seen since the creation of life forms.

They'll be supernatural in origin and made from the material substance of angels, which is awesome and extremely vicious. Only they'll look as John the Revelator describes them to look, or we could say, they'll look exactly the way our Great God describes them.

Especially since the creatures John the revelator saw were the revelation of Jesus Christ, who gave John his glimpse into the future. However, many flesh and blood people have difficulty believing in the supernatural for odd and illogical reasons.

Especially the supernatural beasts, prophesized to come upon this Earth from the pits of Hell during the great tribulation time. Truly, we would be naïve to believe they'll not come here when the gates of Hell are opened. I want you to know that this Earth's surface is their destination.

However, for some unexplained reason, most preachers say that the supernatural beast's description symbolizes machines and armies of men. However, there's nowhere within the Bible where this assumption men make can be verified by any scripture.

Indeed, the scriptures specifically describe them as living beasts from Hell, and they'll ascend out of the bottomless pit. I am certain the extremely intelligent John the Revelator had a good mind, had seen many mechanical things during his lifetime, and knew the difference between living creations and mechanical devices.

I am certain John knew the difference between machines and created supernatural fire and manmade fire. But to each their own opinion, we must choose between the literal and the symbolic, but there are only two choices.

However, the odds of one hundred percent accuracy, coming from anyone's interpretation, is improbable but not impossible. But sticking to the facts we know to be true should be the basis for a calculated assumption on the other things assumed as unknown.

We know that the wicked angelic Lucifer is the king of the bottomless pit, and the bottomless pit and Hell are in the same place. Surely, the demons locked away in Hell would be upon the surface of this Earth right now if God hadn't created Hell for their residence.

Beyond the shadow of a doubt, we do know where the ungodly dead go to live because of the revealing story concerning the poor Lazarus and the rich man. I believe the rich man in the story of Lazarus reveals Hell as a real place where there's no water.

Indeed, the educational Lazarus story reveals ungodly men who've died and gone before you and I are living in the pits of Hell and are still alive in spirit form. This truth means the ungodly dead are still alive and waiting for a release date, and they will return to control the Earth.

Furthermore, because of the angels' indestructible bodies, and because the Apostle Peter says so, we know that the rebellious angels are bound in the pits of Hell and still alive after many thousands of years. This revelation means the pit of Hell is an underground place for prisoners.

Indeed, we know that Lazarus is still alive and living in Heaven, and the rich man is still alive and living in Hell. Certainly, both of them are alive, regardless of their new form, after the death of their flesh.

Therefore, whatever is predicted to come out of the bottomless pit will be a mix of the ungodly and the supernatural bound in the pit of Hell. This truth means during the last four thousand years of being confined to the center of this Earth, with nothing much to do except to improve their strength.

We can be certain the spirits of the damned and the evil angels are wiser than they were and evolved into much more than they were when they first entered Hell. Therefore, if we must choose, our belief must be between two assumptions: created living creatures or machines.

It's for certain; we have the choice to believe the description of these creatures from Hell is symbolic of manmade machines, or we can believe their description is literal and exactly as John the Revelator describes their appearance.

As for myself, I choose to believe their monstrous description is literal, and I believe some will hurt and kill an unnumbered part of ungodly mankind. I also believe they will be here soon, and they'll arrive like a thieve in the night and swiftly take control of the surface of this Earth.

I believe the fierce beasts from Hell John describes in the Book of Revelation are accurate, and nothing about their description is symbolic. John truly describes what's to come upon this Earth during the terrible time of tribulation.

I believe the four angels from the Euphrates River that will assemble the two hundred-million-man armies from the surface of this Earth will be much different than the evil army, which ascends out of the bottomless pit because they do not come from the pit of Hell.

Furthermore, Bible scriptures reveal that the command of God is the voice that releases the four angels bound in the Euphrates River. As stunning as it is to believe, these are supernatural angels, and they'll go forth and kill a third of mankind, but no particular nation is mentioned.

However, we can be certain that they'll go forth to kill ungodly men everywhere living on this Earth, probably from many nations. The most popular theory preached among preachers not convinced that John the Revelator is describing a supernatural army.

It's believed that this two hundred-million-man army is put together from the population of China, Russia, and other allied nations who oppose Israel. But the Bible says otherwise, and I am not convinced they are correct in assuming this two-hundred-million-man army will oppose Israel only.

Revelation 9:16 The number of the army of the horseman were two hundred thousand thousand:

Revelation 9:17 And the horses in the vision, and them that sat on them, having breastplates of fire, jacinth, and brimstone: and the heads of the horses were as the heads of lions; and out of their mouth issued fire, smoke, and brimstone.

Although the Euphrates River will dry up, the Kings of the East will march to Israel. The spirits of devils will go forth to the Kings of the Earth, working miracles and gathering them to the battle of that great day of God Almighty.

Indeed, it's the ungodly people living on this Earth whom this army will kill, commanded to be released by our Great God, and this two hundred-million-man army is put together to slay one-third of mankind regardless of the nation.

Furthermore, it's easy to see that all of Earth's nations are mostly liberal and ungodly, and this analogy includes many Americans. It's easy to believe the ungodly people will be singled out and slayed in nations in every corner of the Earth.

Indeed, I believe this two hundred-million-man army, put together on the surface of this Earth, will not complement the Mark of the Beast army. Mainly because there's another army of rebellious angels and the spirits of ungodly men and women locked away in the pits of Hell, and we better not forget about them.

Furthermore, they've been building in numbers since the first generation before the great cleansing flood, and their numbers will not stop increasing until the great tribulation time maximizes its quota. These two great armies will not be allies, but both will kill the wicked people on Earth.

Indeed, the pits of Hell are not given much thought by most people. Hell is the unaccounted and unthought-of underground military base of the abomination of desolation. I am certain the number of his marks of the beast army is unimaginable and constantly growing.

I assure you, the spirits of ungodly people gone before us are locked away in the pits of Hell, and they probably outnumber the Chinese and Russian populations by many numbers. It's correct to say they are members of the Mark of the Beast army and will fight in the great battle of tribulation.

Furthermore, I am certain that the ungodly spirit people from the pits of Hell have a reason to fight. They'll have a greater motive to kill men on earth, much more so than the Chinese and Russians, even though the Chinese authority and the Russian authorities are ungodly people and kill easily.

The supernatural army, modified and formed from the ungodly creatures coming out of the pits of Hell, might be an enemy to China and Russia. They'll also be an enemy to us if we are an ungodly person, and I say ungodly people because killing the godly person may be hard to accomplish.

I believe the real enemy is formed from the supernatural servants of Lucifer. They'll kill the ungodly part of mankind for pleasure when they find those who do not have the seal of God inside their forehead, and not having God's seal means not having God's protection.

Furthermore, the army from Hell would kill the servants of God if God didn't command them not to or were afraid and unable to kill the sealed believer in Christ. However, in the end, it'll come down between the servants of God and Lucifer, and they'll battle for domination upon the breath of this Earth.

Meanwhile, while locked away in Hell, it's logical to assume that the fierce supernatural army of demons from Hell is readying itself to battle with Jesus Christ and His saints at the second coming. I am certain the desperate army from Hell will fight hard to win a habitation place they can call home.

In the final battle upon this Earth, all of the residents of Hell, since the beginning of time, will fight against the army of Christ for ownership of planet Earth. I assure you they know this is a life and death battle for them, void of the promise of a resurrection.

Furthermore, it could be possible the horses are shaped like locusts and are prepared in Hell for battle, with crowns on their heads, and have the faces of men, the hair of women, and the teeth of lions. They'll be remodified angel forms or monstrous-looking bodies fabricated in the pits of Hell.

I believe the mark of the beast spirits will have fabricated bodies specifically designed for the ungodly spirits of the lost and the damned. The lost and the damned are the unsaved, bound in Hell since the beginning of the second Earth age.

Indeed, whoever ascends out of Hell will be much stronger than when they descended into the pit of Hell, and they'll be transformed into monstrous Frankenstein creations, redesigned in the workshop in Hell.

Surely, after thousands of years, an unnamed angel from Heaven opens the gates of Hell. Then, everyone from every generation who descended into Hell isn't bound permanently from ascending back out of Hell. Therefore, when the gates of Hell are opened, freedom will come to the center of this Earth, and all the evil creations locked away within it will regain the same strength they had before the flood.

Beyond the shadow of a doubt, everyone locked away in Hell will ascend out of the pit of Hell, and having the Mark of the Beast means they'll come out of Hell united against the Son of God and the believers in Christ. It's regardless of the generation; they were incarcerated when they descended into Hell.

Therefore, there's no such thing as permanent death until the time of the lake of fire, except for the death of the flesh. It's for certain: whoever descends into Hell will shed the flesh before they descend into the underworld of the unredeemable.

Meanwhile, as their spirits are trapped in Hell with the wicked Lucifer and the highly intelligent rebellious angels, they'll be transformed into something demonic before they ascend back out of Hell when the gates are opened.

Therefore, I conclude by looking at it logically; it's logical to believe a loop is formed when the gates of Hell are opened. Undoubtedly, the ungodly people alive on this Earth will be killed by the demonic army of the wicked Lucifer, and their alliance with him will make them his servants.

Furthermore, after the ungodly flesh and blood person is killed, their spirit will descend into Hell, and it'll be transformed. After being transformed, they'll emerge from Hell demonic, marked with the beast's mark, and be transformed into fierce fighting creatures.

Positively, everything coming out of Hell will have the mark of the beast, and they'll be a part of Lucifer's army. But there's no way of knowing how long the gates of Hell will remain open until they are closed back, but they will be closed again.

My grandson, Bryan Paul Castle, calls the *Franken Demon Concept The Loop Of Transformation*, and it's because the demonic transformation is similar to the Frankenstein transformation. I guarantee being confined to the pits of Hell for thousands of years has focused the trapped prisoners in Hell's attention on a great prophesized war.

Without a doubt, when the gates of Hell are opened, the transformation loop is the only concept that makes sense because what goes into Hell during the tribulation will come back out of Hell for as long as the gates of Hell are open.

Therefore, the great and terrible tribulation time upon this Earth will be caused mostly by whoever ascends out of Hell. Surely, these next two important scriptures reveal what we should expect to see during great tribulation.

> **Revelation 9:3** And there came out of the smoke locusts upon the Earth: And unto them was given power, as the scorpions of the Earth have power.

The above scripture means these transformed creatures will be stronger than average and hurt ungodly people with their stings, and they'll certainly come to the surface of this Earth after the gates of Hell are opened.

> **Revelation 9:7** And the shapes of the locusts were like unto horses prepared unto battle, and their faces were the faces of men.

Indeed, the fierce beasts from the bottomless pit will look exactly like John the Revelator says they'll look. They'll have hair, as the hair of a woman, and teeth as the teeth of a lion, and the king over them is called the king of the bottomless pit.

These evil beasts are created or modified in the bottomless pit by the angelic demons imprisoned within the center of this Earth, and they've had approximately four thousand years to prepare themselves for their coming battle with the Son of God.

Furthermore, before this unusual revelation story ends, I ask you, are the descriptions written within the book of Revelation talking about manmade machines, or is the God-inspired writer talking about transformed living creatures?

Truly, I do not believe man's mind can imagine these created creatures prophesized to come out of Hell. Furthermore, since they did not ascent into Hell after the time of the great cleansing flood, it's logical to believe demonic angels created the creatures in the pit of Hell.

I am certain men cannot imagine how terrible and fierce these created demons from Hell will behave on the Earth after the gates of Hell are opened. However, be assured they will be here among this Earth's ungodly men and women.

Indeed, once they are released from Hell and standing on the surface of the Earth. They will hurt or destroy anyone upon this Earth who does not have the seal of God written on their forehead. Maybe, during the tribulation time, the ability to choose our God will disappear, and the only ones left will be the tares and the wheat.

During the seven-year tribulation, these beasts from Hell are back on this Earth for the second time. It could be possible that the Christians with the seal of God inside their forehead, who love God, who have resisted the ways of Lucifer will receive the gift of a Christ-like body.

They'll possibly have a changed body, similar to the angels, and they'll be as strong as the demons who ascend out of Hell. For this reason, they cannot be hurt or destroyed by the demonic rebellious angels or the fierce beasts from Hell.

Therefore, if the above analogy is correct, the seal of God protects the saints from harm. Then, the only flesh and blood people on this Earth who'll suffer wrath from the demonic creatures will be the ungodly people who don't have a Savior or a changed body.

Furthermore, I am certain that my Great Creator God will not give the ungodly person upon this Earth a changed body, and He'll not be their Savior. I believe I am correct to say the ungodly person will receive the Mark of the Beast.

Conclusively, I believe the one hundred and forty-four thousand sealed servants of God are the first fruits to be sealed. But after that, multitudes of believers will be sealed and receive a changed body. Thanks to God, they'll be as strong as their adversaries from the pits of Hell.

However, I believe the only way the ungodly person can receive a changed body will be to be killed by the Lucifer-controlled Mark of the Beast army from hell, and after their spirit descends into Hell and undergoes a transformation process.

Positively, I want you to realize this process is called *The Loop Of Transformation*. But this process is reserved for ungodly people only, and it's their only way to receive a changed body, compliments of the wicked Lucifer, alias the abomination of desolation.

If you think these terrible days yet to come are a figment of my imagination, please consider the words of an apostle of Christ, and then imagine the worst things to happen to humanity your mind will conceive, yet the great tribulation will be worse. During tribulation, no flesh will be saved unless the Lord illustrates mercy and shortens the time of the great tribulation.

Mark 13:19 For in those days shall be <u>affliction</u> (tribulation), such as not from the beginning of the creation which God created unto this time, neither shall be (ever again).

Take heed and remember if any man shall say to you, Lo, here is Christ; or Lo, He is there; believe him not.

The wicked one, Satan, comes back first, and in the beginning, he'll appear as Christ and claim to be Christ. Yet, he'll be a destroyer, a deliverer to the fires of Hell, the wolf in sheep's clothing, and not a Savior from the judgment of damnation.

Please remember after the tribulation of those days, Christ and His angels will return and gather His elect from the four winds, from one end of Heaven to the other. Whoever doesn't take the Mark of the Beast and remains faithful and true will live in His kingdom forever. Therefore, lay up treasures in Heaven and live daily by His holy word.

CHAPTER TWO

THE KINGDOM OF THE AIR

This informative story, *The Kingdom Of The Air*, illustrates another invisible and intangible kingdom. Still, it's real and supernatural, and it has residents from Heaven and Hell; day after day, for as long as we live, we are the subjects of interest to them.

However, this awareness story mostly portrays the intangible spirits coming from the realms of Hell, and scriptures prove they are the evil mischief makers of the air. Their design is so stealthy; they cause every evil act in this world, and the human eye doesn't notice their involvement.

Everyone on this Earth needs to understand this awareness story that reveals ongoing domination. After thousands of years, the fallen angels still control unguarded hearts to some extent, and we, believers and unbelievers, are the prey they want to control.

The wicked angelic Lucifer, the Snake Of Old, is the superior leader of an evil gang of rebellious anti-Christ angels from Heaven, and it's easy to conclude he controls the invisible and demonic evil spirits of the air. Lucifer put together his gang in Heaven, and it's expanded like the sea sands ever since.

Furthermore, he's the wisest and the cruelest of all the rebellious angels, guilty of opposing and warring against God in Heaven. Indeed, being an invisible supernatural spirit, similar to a ghost, has great benefits to some unknown degree, including the ability to lurk around humanity undetected.

Furthermore, the wicked spirit of Lucifer and the evil spirits of the other rebellious angels have the power of telepathy. I guarantee these wicked angels are warmongers and want to plant the wrong thoughts into our minds and gain some degree of mind control.

For this reason, we better live by the word of God and keep a clear mind every hour and daily. Our thoughts must be evaluated to ensure our imagination isn't going off the deep end, running wild, and being manipulated by demonic spirit influence.

This exposure story, unusual and important, purposely reveals evil opponents from another realm. The demonic servants of Satan are our opponents and set sin traps meant to capture the minds and hearts of many victims. I guarantee because the world hasn't changed for the better, every trap they set is a sin trap.

This truth means we wrestle against spirit power and aren't even aware of being in the midst of an ongoing spiritual battle. I want you to realize so you won't be passive or indifferent. Spiritual victory doesn't come easy, but it can be achieved if we are willing to glue ourselves to the perfect word of God.

Furthermore, gluing ourselves to the word of God can only be achieved if we possess knowledge from above concerning His righteous ways. Truly, the written advice of God is the armor for our heart and our only protection from being affected by mind control telepathy.

This truth means Lucifer has a secret way of infecting the naïve and understudied people on Earth with unclean and wicked thoughts.

Sometimes, it happens when people do not realize their minds and hearts are unguarded against the invisible dark spirits of demons.

These sneaky invisible spirits, alias evil, and unclean abominations, wait for the moment to enter us. It's easy to conclude they do it through the unguarded door to our hearts, and gaining access to our hearts is their objective.

Positively, it would be easier to think of the evil Lucifer and his demonic army of rebellious spirit angels as if they are a dangerous air-born virus we cannot see with the naked eye. I am certain because they like to kill, it would be wise to consider them a dangerous air-borne virus, and if we do not, they'll control us like silly putty in their hands.

This truth means you and I cannot know where they are because of their hidden invisibility cloak. But just the same, these invisible demonic spirits are our arch enemy, and they will attack us and destroy us, piece by piece until the day death knocks on our door.

Furthermore, the art of invisible warfare, aided by telepathy, makes demonic spirits tough to defeat. I want you to know before we can be self-defense warriors, it's extremely important to be Bible-savvy and have a strong Holy Spirit guiding us from within our hearts.

Our wonderful teaching Holy Ghost is a discerning Spirit, and He knows the type of spirit dwelling within every person. For our well-being, He can prevent them from entering our hearts and minds simply by providing armor and guarding entrance locations.

It could be factual that when we breathe air into our lungs, the airborne virus tries to enter us while we are unaware our defenses are down. Because our enemy is invisible, I believe the Holy Ghost living within us is the only supernatural friend able to keep the spirits of demons out of us.

The correlation I am trying to make between the wicked Lucifer and the invisible demon spirits of the air is similar to an air-born virus, which attacks from hidden corridors cloaked by invisibility. Most people do not realize they have an enemy trying to destroy them, and maybe their ability to work unnoticed and quietly is the reason for their success.

Therefore, the parallel of Lucifer, the effects of the unclean swine, and the invisible demonic spirits of the air are the same kind of correlation. All three are detestable viruses we cannot see with our eyesight or completely understand because of the barrier between them and us.

Indeed, their evil thoughts are planted into us through invisible means, and their invisible spirit may be swallowed and taken internally when the Holy Ghost isn't living inside us. I guarantee our resistance to having thoughts of sin is weaker whenever we bow to the temptation and eat the unclean swine.

Therefore, there is a difference in how their thoughts enter us and their spirit enters into us. This truth means the unclean animals, specifically the filthy unclean swine, are a probable corridor of their invisible spirit. The best self-protection from demonic spirits and their influence isn't a gun, but it's a clean dwelling place inside us for the Holy Ghost.

This truth means the unclean swine's flesh, men, women, and children, sit at the dinner table and consume into their flesh-and-blood bodies has extremely serious consequences attached to eating it and a serious warning to whoever is unaware and will eat it.

The warning is directly from God, and He's the reason the forbidden unclean flesh of the nasty swine is identified as an unclean abomination. Thanks from my heart, our concerned Most High God tells us not to eat its flesh or touch its carcass because the swine isn't an animal He designed for us to eat.

Truly, I want you to realize and know that the perils of not obeying the written word of God lead to the risk of being influenced by invisible demon spirits. You must understand that not having a body or tangible form means they can live within a host person as easily as the Holy Spirit lives within us.

Positively, and regardless of how you perceive my analogy, the demonic spirits are the same as an airborne virus, and they live inside the unclean person when they are not the spirits of the air. The ungodly characteristics men and women exhibit daily are indicators proving that demonic spirits influence many people and control some of their actions.

I fully believe unclean characteristics are passed to anyone through the gateway of an unclean host animal when the wicked and demonic spirits of the air possess it. The old saying, we are what we eat, has a lot of truth attached to it, much more than people realize.

The analogy of this story proves that many people regard bad eating habits more than His infallible word. This truth means when anyone opposes the perfect word of God or does not believe the truth of it and decides His word isn't relevant, they eat the unclean flesh of the abominable swine.

Then their mind is confused, clarity is fogged, and judgment is off base. However, because God cares about you, I want you to know this refusal to obey the written word of God means, to some unknown degree, that the unconcerned person will become the host of unclean characteristics and the host of an array of foolish things conjured up by the untrustworthy imagination results from an unclean temple.

A man's negative qualities they conjure up are given to them by the demonic spirits of darkness, who rule over the kingdom of the air. This truth means the invisible spirits of demons secretly make their way from the flesh of the unclean swine host and into the human host of whoever eats their flesh.

I want you to realize that many of the symptoms of an unclean person, possessed by the wicked spirits of the air, are negative, and negative thoughts will suppress spiritual wisdom, and we will be weakened by the unclean foods we eat.

Therefore, I conclude that spirit-possessed people are observed and significantly noticeable through the actions of their wild imagination, their ungodly character, and their lack of Bible wisdom. Undoubtedly, having a lack of Bible wisdom reveals spiritual wisdom is weak.

Beyond the shadow of a doubt, the character of an unclean person, other than having a wild imagination, will be flawed by imperfections, such as immoral, lewd, carnal, devious, and greedy characteristics. I believe the unclean person will fall prey to many temptations and fail to have an orderly lifestyle.

Furthermore, the unclean person, living with an unclean living temple, cannot be fully trusted to make godly decisions day after day. Without a doubt, unclean people will lose many battles against the invisible powers of darkness, who rule over the kingdom of the air.

Mainly because host demonic spirits will make a man or a woman too weak to resist abominations of all sorts, and abominations of any sort will cause their character to be flawed by ungodliness. I want you to know our arch-enemy promotes ungodliness and uncleanness, and he influences the eating of the swine.

Its certain ungodliness and uncleanness oppose the word of God and is a character flaw deviated from holiness by the will of the rebellious man. However, godliness and cleanness are proof of an excellent Christ-like character, and whichever of these characteristics we exhibit reveals the spirit we are entertaining.

Truly, I want you to realize the beautiful Holy Spirit cannot help a person possessed by evil spirits unless the possessed person cries out for help. Even then, the affected person must realize their plight, humble themselves, cry for help and want to escape the influence of evil spirits.

Unclean people need to work on themselves and clean up their living temple before they can successfully and consistently overcome evil. Everyone needs help from the Holy Spirit before we can successfully resist the temptation of committing negative acts and various abominations.

These next few revealing scriptures will explain how our wonderful Creator God feels about the unclean, and it's regardless of whether it's unclean foods or other types of unclean abominations identified as carnal and immoral. Furthermore, you and I should be scripture warriors and not oppose His words of wisdom.

The next informative scripture also reveals our Great Creator God wants us to try to emulate Him and His perfect character. I want you to know that He's asking us to observe the rules and decrees He made for everyone and has always obeyed Himself.

> **Leviticus 11:44 (**God says) For I am the Lord your God: Ye shall therefore <u>sanctify</u> (means consecrate and keep clean) yourselves, and ye shall be holy, for I am holy.

> **Leviticus 11:44** Neither shall you <u>defile</u> (means make yourselves unclean through the practice of abominations, or pollute yourselves by the things you eat, through abominations designed to defile you).

> **Leviticus 11:44 (**Neither defile) yourselves with any <u>creeping</u> <u>thing</u> (means do not eat anything) that creepeth upon the Earth.

The definition of unclean abominations was certainly given to us by the God of Heaven and Earth, and they are animals disgusting to Him. Indeed, whatever our Creator God tells us to avoid is an abomination, and abominations are the specific things He's always speaking against.

I assure you God is the author of the definition of uncleanness, identifies abominations, and is the Creator of unclean animals. This truth means God knows better than anyone else what abominations are and what aren't abominations, and He reveals definitions of uncleanness so we can maintain cleanness.

The next revealing scripture is simple, direct, and extremely important. It means what it says and tells us the filthy swine is an unclean animal to touch or eat, and the God of creation says so. Yet, most Christians eat it anyway, despite Him advising us not to touch or eat it.

> **Leviticus 11:7** And the <u>swine</u> (alias hog, or pig), though it divides the hoof, and be <u>cloven</u> <u>footed</u> (means split hoofed). Yet it cheweth not the <u>cud</u> (grass); it is unclean (detestable and unfit) to you.

It could be possible the unclean split-hoofed swine is their perfect host animal to invade, and the evil spirits of the air favor it. This truth means the unclean swine is a choice animal the rebellious angels use for an advantage to inhabit the humans since almost everyone loves to eat it. Truly, because it's an out-of-place animal lacking helpfulness to the body, it may be the corridor or the gateway of evil spirits.

> **Leviticus 11:8** Of their <u>flesh</u> (the abominable swine's flesh), shall ye not eat, and their <u>carcass</u> (body) shall ye not touch; they are <u>unclean</u> (means detestable, disgusting, and harmful) to you.

The above seriously important scriptures are a warning from our Great Creator God, and all His warnings are to keep us clean, holy, and strong in spirit. Positively, we are foolish if we oppose His wisdom concerning the unclean and gobble up the swine's flesh.

Therefore, God wants us to know that His warning from Leviticus is a warning to everyone on this Earth, regardless of the generation, and especially, He's warning whoever is tempted to eat the flesh of the abominable swine.

Indeed, if I could make a personal analogy, I had to compare the unclean swine and the wicked Lucifer to any other unclean animal. Then, beyond a doubt, I would compare the swine and Lucifer to the unclean, stinking skunk; only Lucifer and the unclean swine will do much more harm to humanity than a skunk.

Furthermore, I challenge any professing Christian to test the word of God and quit eating the swine's flesh for one year. Then analyze yourself after one year, and see if your thoughts and spiritual manner aren't godly and cleaner, and you've become a better person.

The required reason is that you have to test yourself for approximately one year, more or less, and maybe more than one year. It'll take time for your body to cleanse itself of the substance and the residue of the swine previously absorbed into your organs.

However, when the residue of the swine is gone from you, your living temple is cleaner. Then the Holy Ghost of God will be stronger inside of you, and I bear witness to these words of wisdom based upon the word of God.

The next scripture reveals an invisible force, and the spirit control is exposed by identifying the power and the prince of the air. I want you to know that controlling the air's power is similar to owning an invisible radio station powerful enough to send messages to all four corners of this world.

Ephesians 2:2 Wherein time passed ye walked according to the course of this world, according to the <u>prince</u> (means Satan, alias Lucifer, the Snake of Old) of the power of the air.

Ephesians 2:2 The <u>spirit</u> (means invisible spirit of the air) that now worketh <u>in</u> (means through) the children of disobedience.

The Apostle Paul tells us the power of the air, which means control of the air, belongs to the wicked and rebellious Lucifer to some unknown degree. The above scripture indicates that the air's power controls the children of disobedience to some unknown degree.

Indeed, before we know the right way to keep our living temple clean, which is our heart, body, and mind need to be kept clean, we have to know and understand the word of God. We must believe the word of God and live by the stipulated word of God.

Mainly because the children of disobedience are unlearned and Bible illiterate; it's quite possible, mostly because of their unclean temple. Sadly, because their temple is unclean, the children of disobedience only have a little resistance to the influencing power of the air.

I assure you the whole word of our wonderful God provides strength through knowledge, and wise men seek knowledge about Him. Surely, when they discover His formulas, secrets, and mysteries, they utilize them to their advantage.

I know that the infallible word of God is the measured strength of our godliness and armor to say no to their influence. Indeed, utilizing the knowledge of God will protect us against the air's demon spirits, who want us to become a host inside our hearts.

Therefore, being Bible savvy, wearing God's armor, and keeping a clean-living temple means living by God's word. Truly, living by the word of God will increase our godliness and cause the evil spirits of the air to flee from us.

These next three scriptures ascend to the pinnacle of seriousness and are written for our benefit. They reveal the severity of our battle with demon spirits and the importance of being heavily drenched in the wonderful gospel of our Great God.

> **Ephesians 6:11** Put on the whole armor of God, that ye may be able to stand against the <u>wiles</u> (means schemes, tricks, snares, and temptations) of the devil.

> **Ephesians 6:12,** for we <u>wrestle</u> <u>not</u> (means we fight not) against flesh and blood, but against principalities and powers, against the rulers of the darkness of this world, and spiritual wickedness in high places.

> **Ephesians 6:13** Wherefore take unto you the whole armor of God, that you may be able to <u>withstand</u> (means resist temptations) in the evil day,

> **Ephesians 6:13** and having <u>done</u> <u>all</u> (means used the whole word of God) to <u>stand</u> (against the evil spirits of the air).

The Holy Ghost-filled Apostle Paul is telling us to stand against evil, and this accomplishment is achieved by relying on the perfect word of God, and relying on the perfect word of God has a specific definition. It means for us to fill our minds, heart, and soul with the strong gospel of God.

The loyal Apostle Paul tells us that the strong gospel of God is a shield and armor, and because of its strength, it can stop the arrows of the wicked from piercing us. Our Great God designed His word to stand between us and evil for our protection, similar to a strong barrier wall.

This declaration story is meant to reveal the reason for the chaos in this world I call the kingdom of the air. Truly, this is a warning story, advising us to protect ourselves from spirit influence, and without a doubt, demonic spirit influence is our number one enemy.

This informative story entwines itself with the wicked Lucifer and the unclean abominations of this world. I am certain the origin of all abominations is connected to the invisible spirits of the air. If demonic spirits didn't influence men and women to do wrong, the world would be at peace and godlier.

Beyond the shadow of a doubt, the wicked prince of the air and the other unnumbered evil spirits of the air encourage the practice of abominations. I guarantee their spiritual life's purpose is to provoke sin; we would be foolish to think otherwise.

I assure you, doing the will of our Great Creator God and promoting cleanness and godliness isn't their desire. Encouraging men and women to be ungodly and unclean is their desire, and their influence is designed to keep us from the kingdom of God and destroy our souls for eternity.

Therefore, and for the glory of holiness, cleanliness, and self-protection, we should live by every word of God and fight hard to protect our souls from demonic spirit influence. I want you to know the Ten Commandments of God are designed to protect our souls from damnation and the fires of Hell.

God's great and wonderful teaching word, written into our God-inspired Bible, contains soul protection armor. Indeed, our beautiful, grand, and spectacular Bible should be called the great book of heavenly wisdom or our guidance counselor from the heavens above.

I want you to know we have an inner spirit separate from the Holy Spirit and demon spirits. I want you to realize the Holy Spirit needs our love and protection, and we are foolish to leave our inner spirit unprotected and open game for the hunter of souls.

Indeed, protecting our souls means we'll live by the perfect word of God, and we'll not eat the flesh or touch the unclean swine, mainly because we cannot oppose the beautiful word of God and eat the unclean without becoming unclean ourselves.

Positively, the unclean person isn't doing self-protection and isn't showing enough love for their spirit and the Holy Ghost. Surely, it defies logic why anyone would want to become unclean and not know how it feels to be clean and strong in the Spirit of God.

Without a doubt, most people living on this Earth are born unclean, and they'll live their whole lives with an abomination and die unclean simply because they see no harm in eating the unclean. This truth means the unclean has already caused them to be spiritually blind to some degree.

Therefore, I advise you to clean up your act and quit defiling the temple of the Holy Ghost with uncleanness. Afterward, I guarantee you'll be surprised by your improvement and how much better you'll be every day.

CHAPTER THREE

OPEN YOUR EYES

This declaration story, meant to take a serious look at the general condition of our society, is meant to portray the Real World. It digs deep and reveals my analogy of this world, and my thoughts are based on the positive and the negative characteristics of mankind.

Imagine a nation being controlled by cruel and wicked Satan-influenced dictators, such as Herod the First, Herod the Second, Hitler, Saddam Hussein, Putin, Kim Jong Un, Xi Jinping, and Hamas. Also, imagine humanity's quality of life if these dictator tyrants ruled over all nations and men and women who know and love freedom.

Imagine a controlled world where ungodly and wicked leaders like them control our churches and temples. Undoubtedly, we can be certain dictators and tyrants unconcerned about equality for everyone wouldn't like the doctrines of our Great Creator God or His righteous and beautiful commandments.

Imagine a nation with strange gods and a nation filled with religious deception from the pulpits and deception from our government, including deception from neighboring nations and a large majority of people who surround us numb to our Creator.

Imagine all sorts of ungodly deceptions, regardless of male or female, or the nation we live within, where everyone practices deception for gain as fine art. Sadly, a world epidemic, the false face of insincerity, is being used like a tool against the naïve person.

Imagine the wonderful Son of God being betrayed and murdered by people of religious deception, insincerity, and false witness. Imagine the ungodly rich getting richer and the poor getting poorer, and the gap between the two is miles apart and getting wider every day.

Imagine fairness disappearing among men as ungodliness expands and the rich and powerful do not care much about the poor. Imagine an unstable world where the good is called bad, the ungodly and the bad are called good, and evil men are treated with great respect.

Imagine the holy giving place to the unholy and the clean giving place to the unclean, and it all being done in the name of equal rights. Imagine the righteous person being suppressed by the unrighteous person for the benefit of political correctness.

Imagine a confused world, with men marrying men and women marrying women even though it's not pleasing to the God of Heaven and Earth or approved of by Yehovah. Imagine men and women setting their standards and not caring about God's approval or disapproval.

Imagine the unclean and ungodly homosexuals rising on the world stage and mating with the blessings of state and government officials and leaders even though the abomination they do contradicts the Bible and the natural order of things.

Imagine this world not founded on God's morals and principles, such as the Ten Commandments. Imagine men in authority not caring about the word of God or thinking they know what's best for mankind, and more so than the God of creation.

Imagine a lawless society, with reprobate minds taking their place on the world stage and liberal people in authority having ungodly goals they want to accomplish even if their accomplishments stray away from the word of God and lead men in the wrong direction.

I am certain that the definition of ungodly goals is the same as liberal goals, and I assure you, both goals create a larger gap between our Great God and us since liberal and ungodly goals disgust Him.

Imagine a war of moral values and loyalty to God, Christian conservatives and them losing our cities and nation to the ungodly ways of reprobating homosexuals and to foreigners with foreign gods, religions, and heathen beliefs, and them making the rules for Christians.

Imagine us becoming borrowers to the ungodly foreigners and our nation owing them lots of money. Sadly, to say, imagine us becoming compromising enslaved people in our nation because borrowers are submissive to lenders.

Imagine these examples of things that render us submissive to outside pressure from foreign countries not affiliated with the ways of our Great God. Imagine a world of paganism, where paganism has mostly replaced the word of God with the word of man.

Imagine our free nation, one among the few, founded on believing in our Creator God. Yet, our children cannot pray to Yehovah, the King of Kings, in school and imagine a few ungodly people over-ruling the rights of many people.

Imagine our people and our liberal government making abortion legal as if man's point of view about murder supersedes God's point of view about murder. Imagine a world in distress with perplexity, with the seas and the waves roaring, war going on all around us, and economics worsening.

Imagine all these negative things being a mark of the beast's powers growing in strength and the beast getting stronger and stronger yearly.

Until we finally have a one-world government and a one-world church, both of which aren't built on the foundation of God's word.

If you can imagine all these terrible and ungodly things coming true, you can see them happening before your eyes. Then imagine our Great God coming back soon because all these signs indicate He is coming back soon.

Imagine unconcerned men and women upon this Earth and them living a life and death test in the flesh. But still yet, living carefree for the pleasures of this world. This truth means unconcerned men and women aren't taking the prize of salvation seriously enough.

Imagine love for materialism, and most men and women counting material treasures more valuable than those in Heaven. Imagine people thinking about paper money more than they think about my creator, God of Heaven and Earth.

Surely, if you can believe, all these imaginary things are true and will happen, and you realize they are happening in every nation. Then you have excellent foresight and see the real world exactly as it is without looking through rose-colored glasses.

Truly, this is my analogy of the real world, and my analogy is based on the perfect word of God, as I understand it. But sadly, the liberal and the ungodly person don't have Christian foresight and will not share my point of view, nor will the servants of darkness.

Mainly because liberal and ungodly goals aren't entwined with the perfect word of God. This truth means the word of God and the ways of God haven't any validity with the liberal and the ungodly person.

However, I am certain that a day of reckoning awaits an examination in the future for every person born in the flesh. I want you to know a new world awaits, and sin ends on reckoning day, and it's because God has the final say, and He gets revenge.

This concern story is called *Open Your Eyes* and uses the imagination to reveal things out of whack and not in sync with the natural order. So, you'll know, as I know, that all acts of ungodliness are out of whack and unnatural.

However, before this real-world story ends, the imagination can be our worst enemy if we let it take control of our minds. I assure you not many things are worse than harboring an untrue, self-imposed rose-colored imagination.

This truth means anytime we drift away from the original word of our Great Creator God; then we drift into the territory of a rose-colored imagination. I am certain a rose-colored imagination is a prison, and we will have to fight the demon spirit of the air for a clear mind.

CHAPTER FOUR

RUNNING IN THE SAME RACE

This declaration story, meant to entwine everyone worldwide, is called *Running in The Same Race*. It has one specific purpose, purposely designed to illustrate common characteristics all men share, and it's regardless of color, gender, or nationality.

Therefore, if we choose to, we can call this story the truth analogy because there's nothing debatable in this one-of-a-kind personal-to-me story. Because of certain characteristics, everyone living on this Earth is entwined with this story to some degree.

I want you to know that within this unusual story, *Running In The Same Race*; I'll do my best and try to sum up everyone in the world, regardless of whether everyone is a believer in the Son of God or an unbeliever, not having faith in my Great God.

This impartial story, meant to illuminate a link between all of us, called running in the same race, doesn't exclude anyone. Regardless of our stance in this world, whether rich or poor, race, color, gender, or nationality, or the God, the goddess we worship, or whether or not we have a God.

I assure you, beyond the shadow of a doubt, I'll leave no one out of my analogy. Everyone from the Earth's four corners will be stereotyped in this declaration story because men and women worldwide share some of the same characteristics, but not completeness.

In this equally fair-to-everyone story, called running in the same race, I'll evaluate everyone, not individualize anyone. But my analogy will include everyone from all the nations of the Earth, and for the benefit of equal evaluation, everyone must be included.

Furthermore, after considering the spectrum of achieving success in writing this unusual story, I conclude evaluating everyone as a whole is an exceptional accomplishment. Maybe no other person has succeeded in doing it properly since the beginning thousands of years ago.

Therefore, please take your time and read this equally fair story, Running In The Same Race, slowly, and it'll be easier to comprehend the full effects of its meaning. After reading this story, I assure you you'll be forced to realize all of us are running in the same race.

The world is symbolic of a wilderness, and we humans are symbolic of wild and unclean beasts, and even at our best, we are none good. All of us trapped in the flesh are helplessly flawed, and no person can be perfect.

It's certain we humans are the victims of frailty, and death is the only thing able to set us free and loosen our chains of bondage to hurtful things. The flaws of the flesh are like horrible demons or sharp, hurtful thorns that penetrate and pierce our souls.

I want you to know our scars of abominations will never heal because they are a picture reflecting our sinful past. The things that are done cannot be undone; no more than a bullet can be stopped after it's left the gun.

Life is like a clock, only turning clockwise, and time cannot be turned back, and all the foolish things we've done and the regrets in our life cannot be taken back. Whatever we do today, we'll live with until we die because there isn't a mistake eraser that can erase our past.

Therefore, I conclude that the only hope we mistake makers have in this world of flaws is that the abominations of our past are not repeated. Because we learn from our mistakes, we can be remorseful and use hindsight to shape us into better people.

However, regardless of what we are, life goes on as our future extends, and it doesn't stop until the unknown ends. As one life dies out and ends, another one begins, and this pattern coincides with the natural order of things, and there's nothing we can do to change our predetermined life cycle.

I assure you that God set the life cycle in motion, and we cannot change anything concerning the natural order of things. Assuredly, the flesh will certainly fail us someday, and no man can choose the hour and the day, no more than we can grow wings and fly away.

Our autobiography is written in the Book of Life, with accurately recorded deeds we like and dislike, and no secrets will go untold because everything said and done will be brought to the light in Heaven. I want you to realize you, and I can do nothing to change the events written in the Book of Life.

Indeed, fair judgment cannot be achieved until the heart reveals its secrets, and within the realms of Heaven, the unknown will become known. Please know you are writing your book, and all the secrets hidden within the heart will gain a voice and speak from the rooftop.

I want you to realize that our abominations are the sins of our past and are the bad things we did, unapproved by God. But sadly, to say, we humans are fallible, and as much as we do not want to, we'll all fall short of perfection, and this is a flaw of the flesh.

Furthermore, I am almost certain that if a parallel to Jesus occurred, another hand of the trinity was writing in the sand or scribing on the wall. The great message would say, do not persecute hastily and cast the first stone to see another man's house fall.

Mainly because all men and women are laden with abominations and sins, and everyone lives in a glass house. There's none of us so perfect; we can cast the first stone at another person's house because they've done something wrong.

Right or wrong are our choices, and a doer of abominations is wrong. But our revealing Bible assures us life can be right through repentance and change, with the wonderful gift of salvation to gain.

Positively, the hardheaded and the stubborn, laden with sin, will not pass through the gates where eternity begins. For this reason, flee abominations and seek purity, and do not be a wasted soul; leave this Earth sorrowful and unhappily.

Therefore, I advise you to girt up your loins, face life with a grin, and not be afraid to call the God of creation your friend. For the benefit of perfect fairness, He will be your special friend if you'll reverence Him and keep His required commandments.

This Revelation story, Running In The Same Race, is unique and different. It entwines the facts of life with our frailty, the failures of our past, and the ability to start a new life. Because of these common characteristics, I call this story Running In The Same Race.

I assure you the mercy of God is great, and if He's willing to give His life for us, then we should be willing to carry His cross. Bible stories declare being able to start a new life reveals one of the reasons Yeshua suffered murder and died upon the cross for us.

Beyond the shadow of a doubt, it's His pure and undefiled blood, allowing us to repent, change, and start a new life. I want you to know that if we can be stereotyped a certain way, then being Christ-like is the right way to emulate.

I assure you, picking up His cross and walking in the footsteps of His commandments means His blood wasn't spilled in vain. But we are in vain if we believe we can blaze our trail through this life, do right, and be saved of our own accord. Picking up His cross means we've decided to bond with His gospel and love it dearly.

Therefore, I firmly believe that if we can repay Yeshua for His sacrifice, He would tell us to be hot and on-fire Christians, care about salvation for the unsaved, walk in God's commanded ways, and keep His covenant. I testify it's a terrific feeling to be hot and on fire for the word of God.

CHAPTER FIVE

MONKEYS ON OUR BACKS

This meaningful story, concerning me, you, and everyone else, *Monkeys On Our Back*, is true, coinciding with multitudes of people worldwide. I am certain that because of this world's terrible condition, *Monkeys On Our Backs* are everywhere and close to home.

This awareness story portrays the image and characteristics of unfruitful and idle men who refuse to work and be honorable and productive. This real-life story reveals the challenge friends and family encounter when a monkey rides the back of a loved one.

It could be said that monkeys on our backs symbolize parasites feeding themselves off someone else's labor. These monkeys who trouble everyone around them have a stabilizing problem, like carrying nitroglycerin on an old bumpy road.

Truly, the meaning of monkeys on our backs has many problematic definitions, and I guarantee you monkeys are an overwhelming force in this world today. Surely, because of demonic control, they've become an epidemic worse than the swine flu.

I want you to know that the definition of monkeys on our backs expands and entwines throughout the definition of laziness, drugs, unfruitfulness, slothfulness, alcohol, and much more. I am certain that carrying monkeys on our backs is a terrible strain to carry daily, and it takes thick skin to be a monkey-carrying man.

I want you to know that monkeys on our backs are identified as anything able to impede or hinder progress concerning work, spiritual development, and anything else good in our lives. Carrying monkeys on our backs parallels keeping a bad person around, untrustworthy and ungodly, or living under a dark cloud.

I want you to realize that monkeys upon our backs are bad characteristics, bad habits, negative things, and ungodly things. The more monkeys we ride on our back, the more troubles we'll have throughout the day.

Indeed, the fewer monkeys we have on our backs, the better life will be for us, our families, and everyone we are involved with. Truly, because monkeys are tough, it's a colossal size improvement when we shake them off our backs.

Therefore, I strongly suggest we put on the whole armor of God and guard our backs against monkeys looking to hitch rides on our backs. Mainly because a monkey on our back is an intruder, and a monkey is not a welcome guest or an asset to our life.

This truth means the monkeys on our backs should be treated like something broken and needs to be fixed, similar to broken wings. I believe we'll find ungodly people will always have more monkeys upon their backs than whoever follows the word of God.

Therefore, following and living by God's wonderful word will reduce the number of monkeys riding on our backs. Our God-inspired Bible purposely tells us how to avoid hitchhiking monkeys, and we are wise to listen to God's advice.

Beyond the shadow of a doubt, the wicked Lucifer is the father and the inventor of monkeys on our backs. I am certain that developing and multiplying monkeys is his favorite entertainment type, and if we aren't careful, Lucifer will weigh our backs down with monkeys.

Furthermore, whatever monkeys, and how many monkeys the word of God doesn't take off our backs. Then we'll have to get tough and remove the rest of the monkeys ourselves. Simply because we have an obligation to ourselves, and we are responsible for keeping the monkeys off our backs.

Furthermore, I want you to realize that the excellent word of God is our good character adviser. I know for certain the wonderful word of God is our stain remover and monkey repellant. Because of recorded biblical events, I can tell you that Lucifer hates our God-designed monkey repellant.

Truly, I can't know what kind of monkeys are upon your back because everyone has different monkeys. Although every person with a problem usually knows what their monkeys are, they usually know whether or not they want their monkeys removed.

For this reason, it's up to each individual to overcome, conquer, and remove their monkeys. Otherwise, unfortunate people with monkeys on their backs will carry them around wherever they go until the day they die.

However, I am certain you already know the excellent gift of free will isn't demanding, and it will allow us to take the monkeys off our backs, or we can keep them on our backs. Sadly, it's obvious that some people like their monkeys and fight to keep them.

Anyway, I tell you, it would be much better to carry God in our hearts rather than monkeys on our backs. If we want help and desire to change, the God of Heaven and Earth is a monkey repellant, and we need all the help we can get to keep the monkeys off our backs.

The wicked Lucifer has many alias names, such as Satan, the devil, the serpent of old, and the fallen star from Heaven. But I believe the wicked Lucifer should also be called a monkey on our back since he loves to monkey around with our lives.

Positively, I am one hundred percent certain the wicked Lucifer is an evil monkey, wiser than most monkeys. But thanks to our wonderful and caring God, wiser than him, sincere repentance and change will remove him and his monkeys from our backs.

Positively, if I create a parallel to illuminate a conclusion, then I would say, in many similar ways, that sin has the same definition as monkeys on our backs since both parallel the same destroying effect. This truth means that Sin and Lucifer are killer monkeys, and you are their prey.

I am certain you've already figured out that the monkeys I am talking about aren't climbing around in trees and eating bananas in the jungle. But monkeys on our backs are identified by the characteristics men exhibit through lifestyle, lust, vanity, and bad habits.

Everything considered good isn't a monkey on our back, but living upright identifies with a back not having monkeys. Although everything terrible and evil identifies with a monkey on our backs, monkeys on our backs reflect failure and ungodliness.

Monkeys on our backs add unwanted weight to our souls, and monkeys are too heavy to carry around daily. Truly, if we are wise, we should wake up every morning, shake the monkeys off our backs, and stay away from evil monkeys.

Positively, tears do stream out of our eyes, and our soul silently cries within our hearts because it's carrying too many monkeys. But without having monkeys on our backs, the heart is light, merry, happy, and full of love and goodness.

It's certain many monkeys are found on the backs of rebellious, disobedient, and pleasure-seeking men and women, especially men and women who live outside God's commandments, purposely loosening themselves from the commandments of God.

Many times, monkeys on our backs have a domino effect caused by another person with monkeys on their back. This truth means, many times, loved ones and children have monkeys on their backs, too, and it's because of proximity to ungodly people.

Therefore, I want you to realize we are affected by the monkeys on someone else's back just because of our affiliation with them. Monkeys have a way of jumping from one back to another, the same way monkeys jump from tree to tree.

Simply because ungodly monkeys do not care about the name of the back they ride, regardless of whether it's a male or a female back. I conclude monkeys are indiscriminate creatures and will ride on anyone's back.

Positively, trouble-making monkeys put a strain on everyone around them, and many times, men and women who do not have monkeys on their backs have to ask themselves, are we our brother's keeper, who has monkeys on their backs?

Therefore, I ask you and myself: if you and I are our brother's keeper, who may have many monkeys riding upon his back, should we turn away from friends and family because they have a monkey on their backs?

The answer to the above question depends on how much we want to be bothered by someone else's monkeys, and I am positive there's a limit to our ability to help another person. However, each circumstance is different, and the emotion of love affects how much a person will tolerate.

I assure you it takes a caring person with a good heart and a strong will to help someone with monkeys on their back. But good people try to express patience and help brothers, sisters, neighbors, and friends. Quite often, good-hearted, caring people are hurt while trying to help a person with monkeys on their back.

Positively, monkeys are hard to remove sometimes, and we better be careful while helping people who have monkeys on their backs. Simply because monkeys jump from one back to another back, the same way monkeys jump from limb to limb in the trees.

In conclusion, I sincerely tell you that a back that does not have monkeys is strong. But I am certain that strong backs that do not have monkeys are rare and hard to find, and I hope you do not have monkeys riding on your back.

However, before this Hitchhiker Around the World story ends, I want you to analyze everything you can, use godliness and ungodliness as your formula for evaluation, and then open your eyes to reality.

Now, I'll sincerely ask you, can you see the monkeys riding on people's backs, and do you believe ungodly monkeys overpopulate this unstable world? Do you conclude monkeys are an out-of-control worldwide epidemic spawned by the hunter of souls?

CHAPTER SIX

ARE WE OUR BROTHER'S KEEPERS?

Within this curious story, serious, meaningful, and as important as the sun is to life, *Are We Our Brother's Keeper*? I'll evaluate what it means to be our brother's keeper and the expectation of our Great God of creation.

Some people are compassionate, have a good heart, and care about their brothers' and sisters' well-being. While other people are quite the opposite, they have stone-cold hearts, aren't compassionate, and care nothing about their brother and sister.

Truly, since I asked the question, are we our brother's keeper? Then I feel obligated to answer the question I've asked you. Although I will not speak about myself or reference my feelings, I will use two Bible characters as examples.

Indeed, if Cain asks God if we are our brother's keeper, then it's a good question that needs to be answered. Although I warn you, I may not sufficiently be able to answer the question in the fullness of the definition it deserves.

Every circumstance is different, and some questions are harder to answer than others. For this reason, I will illustrate two example persons and use them to answer the brother's keeper's question.

Furthermore, these two important examples do not fully answer the question, are we our brother's keeper? One of my example persons is compassionate and caring, and He's obedient to the perfect word of my Great God.

The other example person is uncompassionate, rebellious, angry, and uncaring about his brother. The uncompassionate one is the disobedient son of Lucifer, called Cain. Sadly, because love was missing from his heart, the uncaring Cain killed his half-brother, Abel.

I'll reveal the compassionate and caring person later in this need-to-understand story after we find out if the seed of Lucifer is his brother's keeper. This truth means, are the ungodly people in this world their brother's keeper?

Furthermore, when I refer to Cain as the seed of the wicked Lucifer, it's because the tree of knowledge of good and evil is the serpent in the Garden of God, and he tricked or charmed and seduced the naive Eve. Sadly, Lucifer changed the course of this world, and God's plan for humanity hasn't been accomplished, and change will not happen until Yeshua returns to the Earth.

The next revealing scripture portrays a talk between our wonderful God and the Serpent of Old, the Tree of Knowledge of Good and Evil. During this talk, my Creator God voices His disapproval of Satan and takes a hard stance against the evil Lucifer.

The Tree of Knowledge of Good and Evil is a walking and talking symbolic tree from which Eve took the fruit, even though it was a forbidden tree and fruit He asked them not to eat. The tree is as poisonous to our souls as a deadly serpent is to our flesh, and speaking bluntly, Lucifer is as poisonous as a deadly serpent.

I assure you, the Tree of Knowledge of Good and Evil isn't an apple tree, nor did Eve learn about evil by eating an apple. Although the forbidden fruit Eve did take from the Tree of Knowledge of Good and Evil resulted in the creation of the bad seed of Lucifer.

The next scripture reveals God's anger and a supernatural curse is imposed on two bloodlines. Indeed, my All-Mighty God tells the Serpent Of Old He will inherently put hostility between the <u>seed</u> children of Lucifer and Adam.

The next informative scripture, serious and prophetic, will span the corridors of time, and it reveals two seeds, which both started in the Garden of God at Eden. This truth means that the naïve Eve is the mother to two seeds, the wheat and the tares.

> **Genesis 3:15** And <u>I</u> (God) will put <u>enmity</u> (means hostility) between <u>thee</u> (Lucifer) and the <u>woman</u> (Eve) and between <u>thy</u> <u>seed</u> (Cain) and her <u>seed</u> (Abel).

Indeed, I am certain there was an enormous difference in strength between the two brothers, and it's easy to conclude the rebellious Cain was the strongest one, and it was because of his mixed bloodline. Sadly, their attitudes were different, and Cain couldn't control his anger and wasn't peaceful.

Indeed, his heart was hostile because of his heritage, and no hostility was in Abel's heart. Indeed, my Great God said there would be hostility, and the seed of Lucifer, Cain, turned out to be violent and an uncompassionate murderer.

This truth means Cain is not his brother's keeper, and Bible history proves Cain is the unthankful child of an evil, rebellious angel. This truth means it's not characteristic for the children of darkness to be their brother's keeper, and Cain perfectly illustrates this analogy.

In the wonderful book of John, there's an explanation verse that refers to Cain as the child of the wicked one. The wicked one refers to the wicked Lucifer, and Cain is his firstborn, and both their works before the flood were evil. Sadly, Eve ate the forbidden fruit of a cursed tree and became the mother of two seeds, and the son of Lucifer killed the son of Adam.

I also guarantee you, because of the above scripture, the never-ending hostility and the controversial subjects boiling up between the liberals and conservatives today have deep roots, returning to the Garden of God in Eden. I must tell you the sowers sowed the wheat and the tare in the Garden of God; Cain is a tare, and Abel is wheat.

The roots go back to an evil and violent time when our Great Creator God said He would put enmity between His seed and the seed of Lucifer. The history of mankind proves that ungodly tares hinder the growth of Christianity and will not let the wheat live in peace as Cain wouldn't let Abel live in peace.

Therefore, it's within the beautiful Garden of God in Eden, where everything was perfect initially. It's where good and evil works were introduced into this wheat and tare world. Surely, I could correctly say that Pandora's box was opened in the Garden of God.

Furthermore, within the next exposure to a mystery scripture, my wonderful Creator God warns the seed of Adam not to be like the seed of Lucifer and Cain. God is saying, let the wicked live wickedly, but our Great God expects Christians to live a righteous lifestyle.

1 John 3:12 (Be) not as Cain, who was of that wicked one, and slew his brother. And <u>wherefore</u> (means why) slew he <u>him</u> (Abel)? Because <u>his</u> (Cain's) works were evil, and his <u>brother's</u> (Abel's) righteous.

After the cold-hearted Cain slew Abel, God came by a little later, asking Cain, where is thy brother? The uncompassionate Cain answered God back with a smarty remark question and said to God, Am I my brother's keeper?

Translated and analyzed, properly defined, and told straight up. The scripture analogy means the rebellious Cain was saying he wasn't his brother's keeper. Sadly, the analogy of this story tells us that ungodly people rarely try to be their brother's keeper.

My wonderful God didn't answer Cain with a yes or a no when Cain asked if I was my brother's keeper, but why should He have to answer the obvious? I assure you He doesn't condone murder, and the God of creation knew that Cain didn't love or care about his brother.

Therefore, we may not be our brother's keeper to a greater extent, but we are commanded not to harm or kill our brother. Truly, many people today aren't their brother's keepers, but many of them are murderers like Cain was a murderer.

Some men are evil, do wicked works, and follow in the footsteps of Lucifer and Cain, alias the destroyer and the son of the destroyer. But there's another story example concerning the compassionate Son of God, always known as His brother's keeper.

His message to the world was to love one another. He commands us to do good works, shun evil, help our neighbors in need, not look the other way, and refuse to see the oppressed person. Because He loves us, He compassionately died on the cross for His brothers and sisters.

During His short time on this Earth, He removed monkeys off the backs of the sick, the disabled, and the blind, and to be helpful, He removed the spirits of demons from possessed people, and whoever asked Him for healing received help from Him.

Until the day came when the servants of darkness rose and killed Him, just as Cain rose and killed Abel. In many ways, the works of Cain correlate with the works of Lucifer, his father, and Lucifer cannot be called his brother's keeper.

However, the good works of Abel correlate with the works of Jesus. This truth means some of us are compassionate and care about our brother and his well-being. But I will tell the compassionate people in this world to be careful who you call a brother because everyone will not be your brother.

Furthermore, guard yourselves against uncompassionate and cruel people, but help them if you can. But do not be their enabler if they aren't willing to conform to the ways of my great God's brotherhood.

This meaningful story, called *Are We Our Brother's Keeper*, has a message crying from the realms of Heaven and even from the throne of God, and this wonderful message is entwined with love and concern for our brothers and sisters.

This important message comes to us from within the holy and sacred temple of God, the holy ones, and the council in Heaven. I am sure all of them say that we are our brother's keeper to an unknown extent if we are walking in the footsteps of Christ.

CHAPTER SEVEN

HOOK, LINE AND SINKER

This exposure story, meant to look behind the scenes, has a dual meaning and amounts to literal and metaphoric stories. In this story, I warn you that if we aren't wearing the armor of God, the hook in Lucifer's Jaw could easily become the same one in our jaw.

Therefore, and for our benefit too, and because we desire to live godly. Please notice closely and avoid doing the ungodly things that become a hook in Satan's jaw, and a hook in his jaw meant temptations he couldn't resist were pulling him in the wrong direction.

If we have foresight, you and I can avoid doing similar things, identifying with destroying his righteousness and closeness with our Great Creator God. For this reason, I am telling you we'll be blessed to learn a valuable lesson from his rebellious mistakes.

This revealing story, entwining the evil prince of this world, explains the hook in Lucifer's jaw, the reason for his lust, and the things he wanted the most in Heaven. Sadly, Lucifer wasn't happy with his exceptional gifts from God and wanted priceless things he shouldn't have wanted.

Truly, before this informative story goes any further, clarity needs to be established, and the definition of hook in his jaw needs to be explained.

The phrase hook in his jaw means he was overtaken by sinful thoughts, which are a hook in anyone's jaw.

However, I want you to realize our situation in life becomes much worse when we act on sinful thoughts because sinful thoughts are the beginning of doing evil acts. With the greatest concern for your souls, I assure you that every act of wickedness begins with a sinful thought.

I am quite certain scales developed over his eyes, blindness overcame the wicked Lucifer, and his mind became corrupted. Sadly, envy was eating at his heart, and he wanted to be more powerful than my Great God. I must say, his sinful thoughts were more powerful than his resistance to doing evil.

Indeed, his conscience was burned as if a hot iron had seared his desire to be a righteous and loyal angel to God, and the hook in his jaw and his seared conscience illuminate the only way we can explain the evil he did against his Creator God.

Furthermore, the hook in Lucifer's jaw expanded, and after recruit time, it included one-third of the vain and rebellious angels. Sadly, the rebellious angels formed together amid Heaven, and he assembled an army of rebels, all of whom had sinful thoughts.

Indeed, they weren't satisfied with their angel status and verbally and physically opposed God and His obedient, good angels. Truly, it was because they wanted more than a noble position in Heaven, eternal life, and a beautiful city to call their home forever.

They had so much of everything in Heaven; they were spoiled angelic brats. The only thing they could want more than they already had would be for them to be gods themselves and not have anyone in authority ruling over them and making the rules to live by.

Positively, Yehovah is the ruling authority in Heaven, and He always was, and always will be, until the end of time. His rules are absolute and cannot be successfully challenged or redesigned, especially not by created angels and humans of His making.

Without a doubt, and I firmly believe, the rebellious and evil Lucifer was Hitler's example in Heaven, and just like the wicked Hitler, Lucifer was willing to take whatever he wanted by force. Sadly, his heart's desire was amassing great power, and he opposed his Creator.

Lucifer was an unthankful person; the corrupt and defiant angels chose to lead them in their rebellion against God. Sadly, within their vain and foolish imagination, they sought heaven's greatest spoils and treasures to reward their rebellion against God.

Truly, you might think that precious metals, jewels, gold, rubies, and diamonds are the greatest spoils in Heaven, but they aren't. I guarantee that the supernatural Lucifer wanted the grand prize much more than precious metals and stones.

Satan wanted the Living Coals of Fire who live continually on the altar of God, inside the temple of God, and upon the mountain of God. The Living Coals of Fire is Heaven's greatest treasure, and no material treasure will compare to them.

Furthermore, what I am calling the Living Coals of Fire is most likely the God element, the spark of life, and the essence of pure energy. I believe the unique and special Living Coals of Fire may also be the wonderful Holy Ghost of God.

Without a doubt, these Living Coals of Fire, who live on God's altar, are the universe's greatest substance of energy; I believe they are animated and alive. They possess immortality and have greater power than any known substance anywhere within the realms of Heaven.

Although as informative as the Bible is about most things, the Living Coals of Fire is an elusive mystery few men will understand. For some unknown reason, a full explanation of their power cannot be found anywhere in the Bible. For an example of their power, if someone is formed entirely from the Living Coals of Fire, they'll live forever.

Furthermore, the Bible doesn't specifically reveal the kind of substance the Father, the Son, and the Holy Ghost are formed from or where the spark of life came from. Truly, their origin is a great mystery; only our Great Creator God knows the answer to it.

Nor does our wonderful Bible reveal the material from which the living temple in heaven is constructed, but we can be certain it's exceptional and beyond our comprehension. As for myself, I believe the temple in Heaven may be animated and alive.

Furthermore, I believe the Father, the Son, and the Holy Ghost are made from the Living Coals of Fire. To emphasize their value to God, the Living Coals of Fire always and continually live on the altar of God and inside God's holy and sacred temple.

Beyond the shadow of a doubt, the Living Coals of Fire are the special God Element and the Spark of Life, and they can give life to other material objects. Indeed, their supernatural abilities make them highly valuable and sought after by some heavenly creations.

Lucifer was the thief in Heaven, and I believe he was stealing something of great value, and it wasn't precious metals and jewels. However, the scriptures indicate Lucifer was merchandising something of enormous value, and without a doubt, the valuable substance belonged to God.

Positively, there's no logical reason for us to believe Lucifer would want to steal gold, rubies, diamonds, and pearls in Heaven. Besides that, the value of precious metals and jewels will not compare to the value of the Superior Living Coals of Fire.

Without a doubt, the wicked Lucifer was using his stolen merchandise to gain popularity and rebel support for his upcoming rebellion, and his planned takeover in Heaven proves his conscience was seared with a hot iron. As terrible as falling from a rock cliff, it's easy to conclude his vain imagination was controlling his heart.

Positively, the wicked and devious Lucifer needed help from the other rebellious angels, who admired him too much, and I believe bribery was most likely the hook in their jaw. Sadly, for the same reason as Lucifer, they wanted the same kind of superpower Lucifer was fighting to secure.

Therefore, it's logical to believe the valuable and wonderful animated Living Coals of Fire was his greatest motivation for rebellion. The extremely valuable Living Coals of Fire was the primary motivation the other rebellious angels desired.

Mainly because the Special Living Coals of Fire is a powerful power source, and whoever controls the Living Coals of Fire controls life. The special God Element is the Spark of Life and the elixir of strength for every living thing, and because of their value, they live close to the throne of God.

Without a doubt, God's precious, valuable, and powerful throne belongs to whoever controls life, and I am certain that the wicked Lucifer was a power-hungry angel who wanted to control life and death. Lucifer had a monumental ambition; he would not abort.

I believe Lucifer was stealing and merchandising small amounts of the Living Coals of Fire, who live on the altar of God. Indeed, he was doing it to build his army of rebellious angels stronger than they normally were at the beginning of their creation.

Beyond the shadow of a doubt, the Living Coals of Fire have multiple advantages, and they not only give life to different types of material substances. But one touch from them and they'll enhance our lives and give us greater strength, energy, and longevity.

Lucifer wasn't a dumb angel, and he knew that he and the other rebellious angels would need a lot of strength to overcome God, especially if they successfully took His throne, temple, and kingdom away from Him by force.

I am certain Lucifer knew only one substance in the universe could give them the strength they needed to conquer God successfully. But I know they would have to steal it from God first, and being the guardian cherub came in handy, and Lucifer was a guardian cherub.

Most likely, the wicked and devious Lucifer started stealing small amounts of the powerful Living Coals of Fire while guarding the throne inside the temple in Heaven. But as time went by, I believe, his stealing increased.

The golden altar in Heaven probably isn't a small altar, and it's much larger and different than we are accustomed to seeing inside a church building. God's extremely special altar is probably much longer than narrow, with many Coals of Fire living upon it.

The wicked and traitorous Lucifer is overwhelmed by lust for power and determined to take the throne away from God. He probably began distributing the Living Coals of Fire among his rebellious angel friends, or at the least, touching them with the Coals of Fire and increasing their strength.

Otherwise, he may have secretly devised a different plan and disobeyed God, letting his angel friends slip inside the temple of God. Then, he may have allowed them to walk up and down within the midst of the Living Coals of Fire. After the war finally started in Heaven, the rebellious angels were stronger than the normal angels.

Feeling confident, they thought they were strong enough to take the throne, the temple forcefully, and the Living Coals of Fire away from God. I believe the Living Coals of Fire became a hook in their jaw. Indeed, they were overconfident in themselves, and after they were caught stealing off the altar of God, the war started in Heaven.

Lucifer was a rebellious angel, guilty of having a seared conscience. Sadly, he thought he could defeat God and take control of Heaven away from our wonderful Most High God because he and the other rebellious angels helped themselves to some of the Living Coals of Fire.

I assure you, Lucifer and the other rebellious angels were extremely smart before they decided to war against God in Heaven. They knew they needed to enhance their strength to a higher degree and make themselves much stronger than normal.

Lucifer and the other rebellious angels were impressed with themselves because they had multiplied their strength, and thinking themselves to be wise, they became fools. Their sinful deeds and foolish imagination were the hook in their jaw.

I can accurately say that Lucifer, the beautiful and wicked fool, was the biggest fool of all the fools in Heaven, and we shouldn't forget to mention his rebellious partners in crime because the other rebellious angels were foolish, too.

The other rebellious, ungrateful, and uncaring angels were fools for listening to Lucifer's great swelling words and partnering up with him. Even though Lucifer promised them a great reward, consisting of great power, all their troubles started with a sinful thought.

Beyond the shadow of a doubt, all our troubles begin with sinful thoughts, and I assure you, sinful thoughts are a hook in our jaw, too. For our benefit, we better abide by God's word and suppress our sinful thoughts before they cause us to do something ungodly.

Lucifer's lust for power and control overwhelmed his sense of righteousness, and the lust in his heart turned out to be a hook in his jaw and the beginning of his troubles with God. Truly, his unrealistic promises to the other angels were lies, and his lies were conjured up from a rose-colored and foolish imagination.

Furthermore, it's easy to conclude his imagination was evil, and hindsight proves sinful thoughts are at the root of the problem, causing Lucifer to lust in vain for the throne of God. I want you to know that the lesson from this story is to reject and not entertain sinful thoughts.

I am certain that sinful thoughts were the hook in his jaw, which caused him to lust for the Living Coals of Fire, who live on the sacred altar of God. Sadly, to say, the evil Lucifer wanted the Living Coals Of Fire more than he wanted friendship with God.

Hindsight proves an undeniable fact: the lustful and vain Lucifer became the fool in this exposure story and a victim of his runaway imagination mainly because the evil Lucifer was willing to do wickedly to acquire the valuable things he wanted in Heaven.

Surely, this illustrated story, illustrating the rebellious angels and the great power source in Heaven, proves a fact. I am saying an angel, man, or woman can sear their conscience, and through the privilege of free will, they can reject God to pursue a vain life inspired by their foolish imagination.

Truly, vanity and a foolish imagination amount to the same thing as sinful thoughts, and sinful thoughts are the beginning point of evil. Acting on sinful thoughts will pull us away from our perfect God if we allow our imagination to become foolish.

Lucifer claimed himself to be special, and he declared himself to be wise among his angelic followers. Sadly, they must've admired him tremendously, although hindsight proves they were wrong to believe in him. However, initially, it probably seemed like his plan was working, but evil plans usually have short-term success, and Lucifer's plan to overthrow God was short-term.

Bible history proves the rebellious angels made a wrong choice to follow Lucifer, and I conclude his foolish imagination was his downfall. It was foolish to campaign among the other angels and promise them the holy and sacred things belonging to God. Sadly, Lucifer spiraled downward into the image of a shameful angel.

The Bible scriptures and evidence positively reveal an uprising in heaven, and the evil Lucifer and the rebellious angels foolishly decided to war against God. It's easy to conclude that being rebellious in Heaven is a flaw, and Lucifer and the rebellious angels made a terrible decision.

It's quite obvious to me that the rebellious angels became blind fools and foolishly followed a rebellious blind guide. I am certain the followers of Lucifer wore rose-colored glasses created and developed by their foolish imagination.

Their problem occurred when the foolish rebellious angels became blind fools, and it could happen to anyone after they let their hearts be deceived and captured by the beautiful and foolish smooth-talking Lucifer. For this reason, we better be cautious of charming talkers offering us an advantage through wicked works.

The lies and false promises the wicked and deceiving Lucifer promised them became the hook in their jaw, and false promises and lies pulled them away from our wonderful Creator God. In the same way, the forbidden fruit pulled at Eve until she sinned.

Conclusively, I want you to realize that, concerning you and me, the purpose of this explanation story is to benefit us believers in Christ. This story goes beyond explaining the hook in Lucifer, the rebellious angel's jaw, and the reason they are separated from God.

This awareness story reveals what they thought was important enough to separate them from our Great Creator God. Truly, considering all their firsthand wisdom, they should've realized it's foolish to let anything come between our wonderful God and us.

Therefore, it's appropriate to create a metaphor and say, in many ways, we are symbolic of a fish. The hook is baited with foolish imaginations, sin, lust, and rebellion, and when the bait is cast before us, we can bite, or we can refuse to take the bait.

Positively, I want you to know that the hook in anyone's jaw symbolizes anything that can pull us away from our Great Creator God. But please remember, the wicked Lucifer only throws out the bait, and it's our choice to swallow it or refuse it.

Anyway, sin is a hook in our jaw, and it separates us from our Great God. Bible scriptures reveal sinners are similar to rebellious children running away from doing the right thing. Indeed, we are running away from doing the right thing whenever we act on a sinful thought.

Furthermore, troubles between our Great God and us always begin with a sinful thought and a foolish rose-colored imagination. I am certain sin is the prized bait used by the trapper of souls, who wants to pull us away from our righteous God and destroy our souls.

Therefore, I conclude that a hook in our jaw isn't different from a fish being reeled in at the end of the fishing line. But please remember, it's Lucifer using the sin bait. The analogy of this story reveals the ungodly people in this world have a hook in their jaw.

Positively, I want you to remember, and never forget, that doing the wrong thing always begins with a sinful thought. It's for certain: sinful thoughts are conjured up within a foolish rose-colored imagination. Please realize that whenever Pandora's box is opened, sinful thoughts transform into commandment-breaking ones. Everyone should realize releasing evil into the world cannot happen until Pandora's box is opened.

This revealing story, a hook in Lucifer's Jaw, is designed to be about the wicked and corrupt Lucifer and the other fallen angels. But it expands to include you and me, and everyone else too, simply because the baited hook is cast into more places than one.

CHAPTER EIGHT

APPEARANCES VERSUS THE HEART

Indeed, this deep story called *Appearances Versus The Heart* is an awareness and warning story that explores our character's strengths and flaws. This story illuminates our need to be a realist, not naïve, and not foolish enough to take everything for face value.

This exposure story illustrates that beautiful appearances and insincere smiles can be a cloak hiding behind a wicked heart. I must warn you that everyone with a wicked heart is wise enough to cloak it, not expose it, since they know no one likes a deceiver, and wicked men know this truth about the prey they hope to deceive.

Truly, the flesh is the most deceptive thing men and women possess, and it's because a wrapped package hides the contents within it. The analogy of why I say the flesh is deceptive is because the appearance of the flesh doesn't always speak sincerely for the heart.

Therefore, just because the outward flesh is beautiful and the landscape is pleasing to the eyes. It doesn't mean the heart is beautiful; one cannot speak for the other, and as hard as it is to believe, the flesh and the heart can send opposite messages.

I guarantee you that a beautiful heart filled with love for righteousness and the wonderful Holy Spirit of God is much more beautiful, well thought of, and highly prized by our Most High God of Heaven and Earth than the appearance of beautiful flesh.

Sometimes, decoys are quite effective; the flesh is the outward appearance, and its exterior hides the interior of a man and a woman quite well. The outside appearance is easy to read, but a person's interior is a complex mystery no one can fully read.

I am certain all of us, men and women, would prefer to be handsome and beautiful and never grow old. However, observation illustrates that not all outward appearances are handsome and beautiful, and everyone grows old.

Anyway, thank goodness, the outward appearance has no reflection on the heart, even though the cover of the flesh hides the heart. Truly, even the dullest tooth on the saw blade knows that, in the long run, the benefits of a beautiful heart will far exceed those of a beautiful appearance.

This analogy is because our Most High God loves a beautiful heart much more than He loves a beautiful appearance, and the importance of a beautiful heart will always be much greater in value.

A beautiful appearance will not improve a person's odds of obtaining salvation in the kingdom of Heaven. Still, a beautiful heart will increase a person's odds of being accepted and favored by our wonderful God.

A beautiful heart dwells within a pure-hearted person if they have sincere love, not fake or pretense. But a beautiful appearance is no indication, proving the heart is pure. Although exhibited godly characteristics indicate the heart is pure, God loves a pure heart.

Therefore, the analogy of this story reveals that a beautiful and pure-hearted person is much more desirable and honorable than a person with a beautiful appearance. Furthermore, if it were possible to read the heart, the outward appearance might not matter.

Indeed, the flesh wars against the Spirit within every person, and the Spirit has defense abilities if the Spirit is the Spirit of God. But a beautiful appearance doesn't possess any special defense abilities, and without having the Spirit for guidance, the flesh will be prone to sin.

This truth means the flesh has a weakness problem, weak against the temptation of sin. But the pure at-heart person does have defense abilities, and it's because the spirit of demons cannot penetrate a pure heart where the Holy Spirit dwells.

I am certain that the lust of the flesh will most likely be the best reason to choose a person with a beautiful appearance rather than someone with a beautiful heart. Furthermore, because the landscape entices the mind, it's easy to conclude the lust of the flesh is an enemy of the heart.

Conclusively, a beautiful appearance is for eyesight only and offers no guarantees to prevent woes and troubles in this life. But a beautiful heart is a good defense against troubles and woes because God watches over and protects a person with a beautiful heart.

Erroneously, most people think men and women who are fortunate to have beautiful appearances have beautiful hearts. Surely, we are foolish to believe that appearance reflects the heart, and this kind of thinking is false and wrong, and the truth may be quite the opposite.

I am certain that the wrong kind of philosophy on beauty could be the reason for many ungodly relationships and failed marriages. Sometimes, old sayings are just old sayings, and sometimes, they have a lot of truth in them.

Positively, the history of love proves that the old saying, Beauty is skin deep, is one of the most truthful old sayings ever spoken, and if men and women would remember the beauty is skin deep old saying when they choose their mate.

Then, their life would be more pleasant, peaceful, and happy, lasting longer without troubles and woes. Mainly because the outward appearance of beauty is just skin deep, and skin deep fades away like the flowers and the grass, and how dull are we not recognize the natural order of things.

Beyond the shadow of a doubt, it's getting harder and harder during these last days for a woman to get a man's last name. Many women marry multiple times anymore, and only a few take their marriage vows seriously.

For the above reason, many men have concluded an analogy, believing a divorce usually profits women the most. Sadly, divorce profits are usually worth more to many women than their wedding vows.

Before I proceed with this story, *Appearances Versus The Heart*, I want you to be assured that beautiful people have an advantage over the not-so-beautiful. Furthermore, I want everyone to know I am not stereotyping beautiful people as having beautiful appearances, as not trustworthy and honorable.

Therefore, I better make myself clear because there are handsome men and beautiful women in this world, and they also have beautiful hearts. I am sure nothing could be better than having a beautiful appearance and heart, and it would be a blessing.

Although, I assure you, having a beautiful heart is much more important than having a beautiful appearance. The handsome Lucifer perfectly illustrates an angel blessed with beauty; we can use him for this *Heart Versus Appearance* story.

The rebellious and wicked Lucifer may have been the most beautiful angel God ever created in the Heavens above. The evil Lucifer was formed from every precious stone, and his form was perfected within the Living Coals of Fire.

The wicked Lucifer was undoubtedly perfect in appearance, but the scriptures indicate he had a corrupt and wicked heart. However, when his heart was lifted, primarily because of his beauty, he wanted to be the Highest God in the Heavens.

Therefore, it appears that the vanity of beauty was his enemy, and his sparkling beauty and pride contributed to his downfall. This truth means his beautiful appearance seems to be the primary reason he'll burn in the lake of fire.

Indeed, the wicked Lucifer proves when the benefits of appearances verse the heart; in the final chapter, the heart proves to be the best between them. But I fully believe it'll take a wise person to realize this truth, and I hope you are wise enough to realize a beautiful heart is the pinnacle part of our body.

Beyond the shadow of a doubt, a beautiful appearance receives more temptation moments than a beautiful heart in love with the word of God. Furthermore, I am one hundred percent certain a beautiful appearance has destroyed many lives, but a beautiful heart destroys no lives.

Conclusively, this extremely meaningful story, *Appearances Versus The Heart,* makes a clear observation and doesn't give beauty an advantage simply because of appearance. Truly, if we are wise, neither will we give advantage to beauty.

Positively, I want you to know that this is a serious awareness story, and promoting awareness is its only purpose. The analogy of this story is to give more attention to a beautiful heart rather than a beautiful appearance.

It's the wise thing to do, and if King Solomon had been wiser than his reputation projects him. Then, the beautiful Queen of Sheba might not have gotten the best of him. But she did get the best of him, and if we weren't careful, the same thing could happen to us.

CHAPTER NINE

OVERCOMERS

This challenging story concerns everyone looking for the right way, *An Overcomer*. It reflects every person's perseverance on Earth, regardless of race, gender, or nationality, and I am certain the immoral condition of this world proves overcoming obstacles is our greatest challenge.

However, this overcomer story isn't about overcoming everyday obstacles or anything considered tangible. But it's about overcoming mind control and the evil spirits of this world, and I want you to realize that winning the prize of eternal life depends on us becoming an overcomer.

Indeed, we all have everyday obstacles to overcome, and they must be conquered, regardless of their size. But our greatest obstacles are the ones standing in our way of eternal salvation and keeping us from winning the prize of immortality.

Therefore, the obstacles we must overcome within this challenging story will be called mountains. But not literal mountains but circumstances and challenges and whatever ungodly thing stands between us and the great prize of immortality.

For example, sin, wickedness, rebellion, and disobedience are rough, tough, and tall mountains to overcome. Within this story, all professing

Christians are mountain climbers, and it's because they've chosen to take the challenge to overcome sin.

Indeed, all Christians, alias believers in the Son of God, have accepted the challenge to escape the judgment of damnation. The wise among many, the believers in Christ, are the only mountain climbers seeking to win the grand prize of immortality promised by our Great Supreme God.

Beyond the shadow of a doubt, overcomers must lay up treasures in Heaven, which are important to gain. Truthfully, we cannot gain treasures in Heaven if we are coasting through life or are satisfied to stay at the bottom of the mountain.

However, because of my faith in the All-Mighty God, I am one hundred percent certain great treasures await the mountain climbers, determined to challenge the many variables of sin and overcome them through the perfect word of God.

I want you to know faith comes by hearing the righteous word of God, and all Bible-illiterate people who lack Bible knowledge aren't good mountain climbers. Sadly, to say, Bible-illiterate people are passive and rarely ever make it to the top of the mountain.

Therefore, if you and I want to be excellent mountain climbers and overcome the many obstacles of sin, we have to know and understand the perfect word of God and use it as our guide around dangerous obstacles. I want to tell you that dangerous obstacles are alluring temptations like boulders blocking a clear road to Heaven.

The seriously important words in the next revealing scripture are the words of our perfect God. They are precious words; my God speaks to Bible-savvy mountain climbers and overcomers, and the next declaration scripture reveals a great reward promised to overcomers.

Revelation 21:7 He (the mountain climbers) that <u>overcometh</u> (the grips of Lucifer, and the wickedness of this world), shall <u>inherit</u> all <u>things</u> (in the next world to come); and I will be his God, and he shall be My son.

The key word in the above scripture is overcometh, and when we understand the definition of the word overcometh. Only then will we be able to know the mystery of the key to life and be more prepared to win the great prize of eternal life?

The key to eternal life doesn't fit with the definition of an ungodly lifestyle, nor does it fit in with men living carefree in the flesh. Mainly because the carefree and ungodly lifestyle amounts to nothing compared to the wonderful afterlife coming after the flesh's death.

Indeed, the word overcometh is a reference word, and it calls on men and women to overcome sin and the temptation to do ungodly things. Similar to the same way, mountain climbers have to cross many mountains before they can reach the finish line.

I assure you that overcoming sin must be accomplished and defeated in this life before we move onward through the realms of time. Please realize overcoming sin is why God sent His apostles, the prophets, and the only begotten Son of His to this sinful world called Earth.

He sent them here so mankind throughout every generation would be equipped with the knowledge to overcome the powerful grips of the rebellious and sinful Lucifer. I want you to know the keys to Heaven aren't given to everyone, and it will require work on our part to be an accomplished overcomer.

The wicked Lucifer is the terrible prince of this unstable world, and he's an evil prince. Truly, he's symbolic of a snake-infested high mountain needing to be cleared and overcome. Urgently, I am telling you, overcoming him is similar to killing the snakes on the mountain.

The great and excellent God-inspired Bible we have today is irreplaceable since it contains the most precious and valuable reading material on this Earth. Indeed, we are foolish if we neglect His reading material and do not educate ourselves in His gospel.

Positively, I am certain that His wonderful and precious Bible is the only book ever written containing the knowledge to help men and women become wise enough to know the expectations of our Great Creator God.

The great Bible is the only book in this world, spanning backward through the corridors of time to the beginning of creation. Thanks to God, it's the only perfect book from our past, compelling men to overcome Lucifer's sinful and wicked ways.

Throughout the scriptures and all the story examples God and men of God have written within the Bible, between the great book of Genesis and Revelation, infallible wisdom is expressed in a way the mind cannot imagine or believe possible for anyone to accomplish.

I want you to know our Great Creator God laid out His plan for salvation, and He wants everyone to know the kind of character He expects in return for the gift of eternal life in His kingdom of paradise. I warn you: His beautiful plan isn't optional, and everyone should conform to His Ten Commandments.

I assure you that winning the gift of salvation is the reason so much emphasis on commandment keeping is written in the scriptures. The excellent Book of Revelation tells us to him that overcometh, he shall inherit all things.

Indeed, I want you to notice the absolute word of God closely; my great God speaks through the scripture in Revelation 21:7. It means anyone able to overcome the curse of sin shall be His sons and daughters, and He will be their God forever.

Furthermore, be wise enough to recognize the meaning of the scripture, and please absorb into your heart the extremely serious message it implies. Mainly because the scripture doesn't say everyone will inherit the beautiful kingdom of God.

Nor does the scripture say everyone will be His sons and daughters, and He doesn't say He'll be everyone's Savior, God. But our wonderful and Great God purposely tells us exactly what He means and uses the word overcometh for a specific reason.

Mainly because the important word overcometh divides the overcomers from worldly conformers, and I want you to know worldly conformers harmonize with the world of the ungodly. Please realize if we blend into their way of life, we aren't overcomers.

Therefore, the word of my God of Heaven and Earth reveals that all of us living in the flesh must overcome the lust of the flesh and the powers of Lucifer, especially before we can inherit the kingdom of God and be called one of His special children.

Surely, the only way we can be overcomers is for us to know the will of God, and His will is written throughout the scriptures within the Bible. God is our supreme Judge, and I want you to realize that Earth is our testing ground, the central location between Heaven and Hell.

I am certain because the order of things never changes that test ground Earth is a designed place where all men and women living in the flesh are tempted. Truly, while living here in the flesh, we'll find out if we can overcome sin's wild and rebellious ways.

Not only do we have to overcome the wicked and rebellious ways of Lucifer, alias our wicked enemy, the uncompassionate devil. We must also learn to be obedient to our wonderful Creator God, who is responsible for creating us from the dust of the Earth.

Positively, expected obedience to His word is why He gave us His perfect Ten Commandments and His many righteous decrees. We can be accomplished overcomers and great mountain climbers through our belief in obedience to His word.

His ultimate test of obedience could be as simple as the holy and supernatural seventh-day Sabbath Day. The seventh day, Sabbath Day, will test the obedience of all Christians throughout every generation until the end of time.

Indeed, suppose we want to be sons and daughters to our wonderful Most High God and overcome the wickedness of this world. In that case, we'll need to utilize the supernatural life-preserving Ten Commandments of God every single day we live in the flesh body.

Keeping all His great commandments means we must keep His supernatural and hallowed seventh day, Sabbath Day, and I must ask myself and everyone else for clarification and correctness concerning obedience to the commanded word of God.

How can a professing Christian in love with the beautiful word of God fully overcome the grips of Lucifer, alias the destroyer of many souls? If they do not focus on the God of creation and strive diligently to keep His perfect Ten Commandments.

I assure you, God's perfect commandments He wrote on Mount Sinai include His holy, sacred, and blessed seventh-day Sabbath Day. I am certain His holy rest day Sabbath Day commandment is as serious as any of His other nine commandments.

However, you and I, or any other professing Christian, aren't overcoming the ungodly ways of Lucifer and the traditions of men contrary to the word of God *if* we show no regard for the required commandments of God and His seventh-day Sabbath Day.

I am certain the mountain we climb to prove ourselves an overcomer means we boldly reject Lucifer's wicked and rebellious ways and the manmade traditions of men. For the benefit of clarification, overcomers desire the truth and scripture authenticity from teachers and preachers.

Therefore, being an overcomer means we haven't conformed to the corrupt ways of Lucifer or the sinful ways of ungodly men. Surely, being a loyal Christian means ungodly ways do not impress us, and being an overcomer means we abhor all acts of ungodliness.

Positively, being an overcomer means we do not bow down to counterfeit religions, and we do not fear other gods. But being an overcomer means serving one God and living by His excellent life-saving commandments.

> **Revelation 21:8** But the <u>fearful</u> (means anyone afraid to stand against the ways of Lucifer), and the unbelieving, and the <u>abominable</u> (means the cursed,) and the whoremongers, and sorcerers, and idolaters, and all liars,

> **Revelation 21:8** shall have <u>their</u> <u>part</u> (their inheritance) in the lake which burneth with fire and brimstone: The <u>second</u> <u>death</u> (coming after the death of the flesh).

The perfect word of God is truthful and a sure word, spoken with the strength of iron. This truth means His words of iron cannot be broken, nor can man's foolish desires change their meaning.

I assure you, we all have the power to be an overcomer if we make the perfect word of God the desire of our heart. But please remember, wherever our heart is focused, our treasure will also be the center of focus. Therefore, I warn you, God reads our hearts' thoughts and knows our attention's focus.

This challenging story, concerning everyone looking for the right way, *Overcomers*, is a metaphor story. But it gets straight to the point concerning our challenges in life, and it doesn't beat around the bush with the needed word of God.

Therefore, neither am I beating around the bush. I am telling you, we cannot be an overcomer unless the excellent word of God is the treasure of our hearts, and as sure as the sun rises every morning, we will have to fall in love with the word of God before it's valuable to us.

I pray you'll be a great mountain climber for the glory of God, and because life isn't always smooth sailing, we will stand at the bottom of many mountains. Therefore, we won't be an overcomer if we aren't determined mountain climbers.

Positively, this reality story says the challenge is to climb all the mountains in your life and claim victory over them, and not be stopped by any obstacle until your feet are firmly planted on the top of the mountain.

CHAPTER TEN

UNCHANGEABLE

This sad story, paralleling a lost condition of the soul called *Unchangeable*, reveals a Satan-imposed heart disease. On a scale of one to ten, it exceeds the long-term terribleness of all other diseases. Sadly, to say that, unchangeable entwines with the spiritual condition of unbelief.

This revealing story illustrates the chief priests, Pharisees, and whoever denies God. Sadly, whoever rejects conversion to Christianity and refuses to believe in the wonderful Son of God will not receive the gift of immortality and live in the kingdom of God. Bible scriptures reveal that He performed miracle after miracle for needy people, yet the chief priests still hated Him anyway.

This story is about Jesus, but it's also a profound story full of intellectual depth and pivots on straightforward and absolute truth. The analogy of *Unchangeable* means some men will not fear God and change and always will be the servants of darkness for one reason or another.

This unchangeable exposure story illustrates a Lucifer-imposed disease of unbelief, and unchangeable unbelief hasn't any connection to a physical disease, a health impediment, or something medicines will cure.

However, this serious story reveals God's wonderful Son curing and healing a blind man, doing good works, and teaching the wonderful word of God wherever He traveled on this Earth. Bible history reveals He spent His entire life advancing the gospel of God and claiming His promise of eternal life is ours if we want it.

Truly, I am certain no one knows how many unrecorded miracles the compassionate Son of God accomplished while being alive in the flesh. But I am willing to believe it was many more than we've been told.

Indeed, with so many blind men being healed and receiving their sight when the Son of God appeared, miracles were being revealed in public. The corrupt Pharisees and the chief priests would not change; they were still unchangeable, mainly because the invisible evil spirits of the air were influencing and controlling their minds.

Truly, after all the divine accomplishments they saw the compassionate Son of God do, they were still corrupt and living their lives submissive to the powers of darkness. After observing Him heal many times, they were still loyal servants to Lucifer, alias the God hater from Heaven.

Undoubtedly, no number of miracles and healings could soften their wicked, unchangeable hearts or open their blind eyes to the truth. It's easy to conclude their conscience was seared with a hot iron, and the truth becomes invisible when the eyes refuse to see.

Furthermore, and I hate to say, unchangeable blindness still exists today, and there doesn't seem to be a cure for a flawed heart suffering from unchangeable unbelief. Truly, we can lead a horse to water, but we cannot make the horse drink, no more than cure unchangeable unbelief.

The above analogy means nothing could compel the Pharisees and the chief priests to love and accept the wonderful Son of God as their Savior from the judgment fires of damnation. I warn you and everyone living on the Earth that the flaw of unchangeable unbelief will result in damnation.

Not anywhere within the scriptures have I found one word saying: the chief priests and the scribes cried out and said, Hosanna, Hosanna to the Son of God. Nor did they say, save us, we pray. Sadly, it's still the same today, and this behavior illustrates unchangeable unbelief.

Still yet, someday in the near or the distant future, after the death of the flesh. Every person suffering from unchangeable unbelief will discover that no man will see the Father without seeing His Son first. After the temptations in this world cease to exist, and nothing is left but our souls, it will be too late to accept a Savior.

The next scripture proves the chief priests and the scribes were eyewitnesses to the miracles performed by Jesus. I want you to know that being an eyewitness is solid proof, proving the truth, but we've seen it too many times; the spirit of unbelief is unchangeable, especially if supernatural accomplishments cannot compel a person to believe in the wonderful Son of God.

> **Matthew 21:15** And the chief priests and the scribes saw the wonderful accomplishments (means miracles) that Jesus did, and the children crying in the temple and saying <u>Hosanna</u> (and the word Hosanna means, save us, we pray.

This truth means the word Hosanna is an exclamation or a shout of praise to the wonderful and helpful Son of God. This exclamation of faith in Hosanna expresses concrete belief in Yeshua. However, some people believe in Him with all their hearts, and nothing can convince others to believe in Him.

> **Matthew 21:15** and <u>they</u> (the believers inside the temple) cried saying, Hosanna to the son of David; and <u>they</u> (the chief priests, and the scribes) were <u>sore</u> (means extremely angry, and bitterly) displeased.

Indeed, at the temple in Jerusalem, where the wonderful Son of God was teaching the crowds of hungry believers in God. The chief priests and the scribes hated hearing the crowd call Jesus Hosanna, even after watching Him do incredible miracles.

Therefore, it seems conclusive to believe and say it must be factual when the eyes see and the ears hear. But sometimes, perception of sight and sound is lost because of unbelief, and the facts are dismissed because of an uncaring attitude.

Beyond the shadow of a doubt, unbelief is an unchangeable worldwide problem that is seemingly insolvable and negatively affects the heart and soul. Undoubtedly, unbelief in the Son of God causes blindness to the truth and deafness to righteousness and holiness.

Although I am certain that the wonderful and Supernatural Son of God could've healed His enemies of their unbelief and spiritual blindness, I know He could've cured them of spiritual deafness.

However, if He did cure them of their spiritual blindness, deafness, and unbelief, then He would've been forcing His will on the loyal servants of Satan, and He would've been taking away their free will. I want you to know my righteous God isn't a tyrant, and He doesn't force everyone to live godly, but He will not let everyone live in His kingdom.

Therefore, when ungodly men defy logic, the greater light will not enter them, and they purposely oppose Him and His good works and cannot force themselves to believe His words because they are wicked tares, and an unseen force controls their nature.

I guarantee the unseen force is the wicked guiding spirit of Lucifer, or it's one of his many demon angel friends. Whenever a person suffers from unchangeable unbelief, we can be certain we've crossed paths with a servant of a wicked guiding spirit.

However, for the first time in their lives, since the day they became men, the chief priests and the scribes saw holy things happen; they had never seen happen before. But, the miracles they saw didn't matter to them, mainly because they were unchangeable of unbelief, and seeing miracles will not heal the unchangeable or soften their hearts.

By all means, the chief priests and the scribes should've been pleased to witness the great miracles accomplished by the wonderful Son of God. Especially after seeing the Son of God perform miracles, break the odds of being lucky, and heal many afflicted people of various diseases.

The chief priests and the scribes should've repented and joined themselves to Him and gladly started sharing God's wonderful gospel wherever they went. Truly, this is what all people do after the light enters our hearts and we become loyal believers in Christ.

Positively, *if* their sight was good, and their ears could hear, without hate and unbelief causing blindness of the heart. Then they, without suffering from spiritual impairments, would've loved the wonderful Son of God and the life-saving gospel of God.

Without a doubt, they would've cried out to the wonderful Son of God and said, Hosanna, Hosanna, save us, we pray. Because someday, we'll all say, Hosanna, Hosanna, save us, we pray. I want you to know there will come a time and a day when the scales fall away from our eyes.

However, they didn't cry out, and they didn't say, Hosanna, Hosanna, save us, we pray. Sadly, it was mainly because of their unchangeable blindness, deafness, and unbelief, including an unchangeable wicked heart. Sadly, an invisible guiding demon spirit influenced unbelief, and they couldn't overcome the power of Satan.

I am certain that this kind of terrible condition I've just described means they were unchangeable people, uninterested in being healed of spiritual blindness and the curse of unbelief. Sadly, to say, incurable unbelief is a terrible condition of the heart, unrepairable in many cases.

Suppose any event can soften a hardened heart, open blind eyes, and deaf ears, and turn unbelief into belief. Then, it would've been the genuine miracles and the genuine worship they witnessed in the temple of Jerusalem when the Son of God was present.

Had they been wise temple priests and scribes, they would've asked Jesus to forgive them of their unbelief, but they were unchangeable. Sadly, Bible history proves the chief priests and the scribes didn't ask the wonderful Son of God to forgive them and heal them of their unbelief.

Had they been wise temple priests and scribes, they would've bowed on their knees and asked the wonderful Son of God to forgive them of their hypocrisy. Hypocrisy means they were acting like men of the cloth and purposely being insincere in the house of God.

However, it's easy to conclude they wouldn't change their corrupt walk with the wicked and rebellious Lucifer. Furthermore, I am unaware of any scripture within the Bible saying they converted to a loyal believer in Christ and decided to walk with God.

Therefore, I believe the chief priests and the scribes preferred to stay unchangeably blind, deaf, and numb to the truth. The story about them in the New Testament indicates they chose to keep their hardened hearts and hate for the Son of God and be unchangeable.

Sadly, regardless of the evidence contrary to their unbelief, they couldn't see a Great Savior standing among them. This analogy statement means the wicked Lucifer found their weakness and encased them in an invisible barrier, blocking the truth from rescuing them from him.

Indeed, they weren't moved or impressed by the many miracles and healings they witnessed the wonderful Son of God do for all the people around them. Because they didn't care, I firmly believe they are unchangeable if the Son of God cannot inspire a person to repent and change.

The great gift of salvation through repentance was within their grasp, and all they had to do was open their eyes and believe in the wonderful Son of God. But sadly, to say, their heart was hardened, and they couldn't, or wouldn't believe in Him.

This truth means they were so spiritually blind by unbelief they let conversion to Christianity, entwined with salvation, pass them by. It was mainly because of their misplaced loyalty to the Roman authority and the wicked prince of this world, Lucifer.

It was extremely sad, evil, uncaring, and uncompassionate for the chief priests and scribes to hate the wonderful Son of God so much. They hated Jesus so much they didn't want to see the lame person walk, the blind to see, or the ungodly converted to Christianity.

I assure you, no one can hate the Son of God, reject the miracles of God, and still claim salvation and have a love for God. This truth means we either believe in, do not believe in, hate, or love the wonderful Son of God.

It's certain: Belief or unbelief between God and us is what it all boils down to concerning the analogy of our decision. It's easy to conclude being an unchangeable believer is highly acceptable to God, but unchangeable unbelief in the Father, His Son, and the Holy Ghost of God is unacceptable.

This truth means you, me, and everyone else will end our lives as believers or unbelievers. However, the spiritually blind person will not realize it until it's too late to repent and change. As we walk through this life, we all must choose to reject or accept the Son of God.

Positively, the chief priests, scribes, Pharisees, and many others who suffered from the curse of unbelief had the same choice as us. But a hardened heart is without compassion for other people, and haters of the gospel of God have an unbelieving heart.

Furthermore, a hardened heart may be unchangeable without believing in the Son of God. However, to preserve our soul, when the Spirit of God comes calling on our heart, we better ensure our heart is soft enough to see, hear, and believe in Him.

This revealing story, as serious as a heart attack, concerning the unbelievers in this world, is called *Unchangeable*. It's both an awareness story and a warning story, entwined with another story from the New Testament, and it includes the chief priests, the scribes, and Jesus.

The story from the New Testament pretty much proves unbelief is unchangeable, especially if we are willing servants of Satan, enjoy the pleasures of sin, and suffer from unbelief. Truly, everyone needs to know that the common denominator among Lucifer's servants is unbelief in God.

This unnecessary sad story, *Unchangeable*, entwines the illogical stance of unbelief. But this story should stir up our curiosity concerning the reason some men believe in God and the reason some men do not believe in God.

Indeed, in our corrupt world today, many people suffer from supernatural curses, and some are born a certain way. For this reason, we should ask ourselves, why does it seem like some people are born with an ungodly disadvantage, different from normal?

Furthermore, and for the benefit of being wiser, we should seek to know the reason; some men and women believe in our Creator God easily. We should want to know the reason; some men refuse to believe in the validity of God, regardless of any reason.

Indeed, I want you to know the answer might have originated in our past. Either from a previous Earth age, before the great cleansing flood, or even further back to a heavenly age, when we knew God from before. Undoubtedly, if we evaluate the reason, as of here and now, then the answer will elude us.

I assure you, this existence we live in now isn't our first time because our Great and Wonderful Creator God knew us all from the foundation of this Earth. This truth means you and I have an unknown history; our minds cannot recall after exiting the womb.

Furthermore, I want you to know that this Earth's foundation is old, and it began during the Ancient of Days and possibly billions of years ago. Unknown to us, there was the age of the dinosaurs, and afterward came the rebellious angels from Heaven and then the flesh and blood humans.

This truth means, unbeknownst to us, who live in the flesh, our belief or unbelief in God has a long history. Even though we aren't aware of our history, God is aware of it, and our desire to believe in Him or not believe in Him is connected to how we lived a previous life.

Therefore, I firmly believe our belief, or unbelief, could be inherited from another time, and the unbelievers who refuse to believe in God suffer from the disciplinary punishment of a supernatural God-imposed curse. Maybe, they suffer from a God-imposed curse because they received not the love of the truth; they are given a strong delusion to believe a lie and be damned.

Bible scriptures reveal, and I firmly believe, that we aren't totally in control of all our circumstances. Not any more than King Nebuchadnezzar was in control of his seven-year curse imposed on him by our great all-mighty God and other heavenly creations.

I assure you the supernatural curse imposed on King Nebuchadnezzar caused him to suffer through personal hardships for seven years. The King's curse proves supernatural creations can and do control our minds and hearts sometimes, but to an unknown degree.

Therefore, I assure you that God and the holy ones in Heaven have power over our minds, and for perfect fairness, they will accomplish whatever they want. This awareness means, to a great extent, our calling into the family of God and our belief in Him, without having visual proof, may have a supernatural origin.

Furthermore, whoever suffers from the curse of incurable unbelief may also have a supernatural problem originating from the Heavens above. I want you to know the great gift of free will and the price tag for sin may entwine together until all sin debts are paid.

Beyond the shadow of a doubt, we may never know the extent of our free will and the extent of spiritual control. However, never say tomorrow; if we receive a calling from God, we better accept it immediately and be thankful for getting a call from our Great God.

Indeed, I advise you that accepting His calling to be a family member in His kingdom is the only logical thing to do, and turning our calling down is a fatal mistake. It illustrates a sign of unchangeable unbelief, a foolish frame of mind, and a careless attitude toward our souls.

Furthermore, we may not receive another opportunity to claim salvation and be a confirmed child of God because options will disappear sometimes. This truth means if we miss our opportunity and we do not believe in God before we die, then we'll have to face God on Judgment Day while suffering from unchangeable unbelief.

Before I finish this story, I want to tell you the conclusion to the whole matter, and you'll know the duty of man. Please realize that being a new man in Christ means we'll do the will of God to the best of our abilities and conform our lifestyle to His perfect Ten Commandments.

Remember, we have a covenant with the God of Heaven and Earth, and He expects you and me to keep His commanded agreement. No desire to keep the Ten Commandments covenant means we aren't His children, and He knows us not, and a life of immortality we'll not receive.

CHAPTER ELEVEN

COASTING THROUGH CHRISTIANITY

This personal observation story concerning believers in Christ, *Coasting Through Christianity,* is profound and meant to increase intellectual understanding. This story reveals the difference between coasting and being a devout believer in the ways of God.

This revealing story isn't meant to step on anyone's toes or hurt anyone's feelings. But this is a parallel story to the sword of the Lord, and the truth matters. As intended within this story, the sword cuts whoever is under its blade, and the truth is a sharp blade, the sword of the Lord.

Therefore, coasting through Christianity is risky, and coasting may cause the God of creation to be unhappy with some Christians. Please realize because of a lack of enthusiasm, our Great Creator God may not be pleased with a passive Christian and draw His sword on coasters.

This truth means that if you are a professing Sun-day Christian, you're content to sit in the pews and accept whatever comes from behind the pulpit as absolute. If you do not hunger enough to know for certain if the preaching you hear is the real gospel truth of God.

It illustrates your feelings and reveals that you aren't eager enough to know more about our All-Mighty God than just bits and pieces and simple mainstream information. My Almighty God wants us to know more than bits and pieces about Him, and we are foolish to avoid learning His word.

Furthermore, if you are coasting through Christianity and aren't an enthused studier of God's wonderful word He's given to you and me, I am prone to believe your knowledge about Him will be lacking. Higher learning will elude you, and you'll fail to understand His character.

Therefore, you'll fail to know God as thoroughly as you should, and we should try to know Him extremely well. However, it may be impossible for anyone to have a close personal relationship with Him as long as they are coasting through Christianity.

I assure you, coasting through Christianity will not be nearly as satisfying as riding high through a life of Christianity. Sadly, to say, the majority of professing Christians are coasting through Christianity, similar to a car nearly empty of gas or a sailboat without wind.

I believe, at the end of our odyssey, as we proceed through the world of Christianity, toward our end time in the flesh body. We'll all wish we would've been on fire for the beautiful word of God, like the fiery cloven tongues at the Pentecost Revival.

Indeed, I prefer not to waste my time being a boring passive Christian, content to coast to Heaven. But I want to enter into Heaven with a history of good works or like a man on fire, similar to a fireball, who opposed Lucifer and acts of ungodliness to the fullest extent.

I do not want to live my life nor end my life of Christianity in a rocking chair, waiting for the death of the flesh. To find out from my wonderful God of Heaven and Earth my life in the flesh was wasted in vain because I wasn't on fire for His word.

Therefore, when I die and the angels come for me to carry me back to Heaven, I would rather carry them back to the Kingdom of God. But for now, while we are vibrant and alive, we have the choice to oppose and expose counterfeit Christianity strongly.

Therefore, we should demand that our churches embrace and conform to the exact word of God. Because we understand His covenant, we can be certain our God of Heaven and Earth wants authenticity practiced in His churches.

I assure you, and you need to realize that coasting through Christianity isn't strong Christianity. Sadly, it's easy to conclude that Christian coasters do not have enough salt running through their veins, a strong enough backbone, or the will to be similar to an oak tree standing against the wind.

Furthermore, it's vain to think that weak Christianity can stop the devil's wiles from replacing the word of God with the traditions of men. These next few revealing scriptures are the words of Jesus Christ, taken from the book of Mark in the New Testament.

Furthermore, I assure you the next scripture reveals important words of wisdom, and the message is relevant to answered prayer requests. In these next few extremely serious scriptures, Jesus speaks important words and their meaning; remembering them will benefit us daily.

The words He speaks specifically illuminate weak Christianity and a failure to keep the traditions of men out of the house of God. These next few warning scriptures reveal the consequences of neglecting to study the word of God and mindlessly coasting through Christianity.

Mark 7:7 How it's in *vain* (means you are wasting your time, and in vain) do they (means Christians, who keep the traditions of men) worship Me (Jesus),

Mark 7:7 teaches for <u>doctrines</u> (means the traditions of men, contradicting the word of God in favor of) the commandments of men.

The above serious words are the words of Yeshua, the Son of God, and He is our wonderful Savior from the fires of Hell. He tells us it's vain for you and me to think we can be an acceptable Christian if we keep the manmade commandments of men.

The meaning of vain worship is wasted worship on something contrary to the word of God, and vain worship hasn't any effect on our Most High God. I assure you the teaching and the keeping of the counterfeit traditions of men will rob Christians of pure and undefiled worship.

Indeed, it pleases Lucifer extremely well when he observes professing Christians coasting through Christianity. This truth is because coasting through Christianity is similar to going too slow in a moving vehicle and taking too long to reach our destination.

Undoubtedly, coasting through Christianity, Christians are asleep Christians. Sadly, to say, they'll not see the traditions of men as a harmful and ungodly gospel, and for this reason, I warn you: Lucifer searches the world to find sleepy Christians living too relaxed in His word.

Coasting through Christianity, Christians aren't Bible savvy and cannot be effective watchmen on the wall. Nor are they wise enough and caring enough to prevent the devil's doctrine from being grafted in and observed in the wonderful house of God.

Extremely important, and never forget, Christians can make the word of God of no effect if they replace the word of God with the traditions of men. Surely, if Christians make the word of God of no effect, then all the faith in this world will not help them receive answered prayers.

Therefore, if you say, I am standing on the word of God, or if you say, I have faith, but you keep the traditions of men. Then, sadly, I must tell you, you still make the word of God of no effect, regardless of whether you realize it or not. Like a self-inflicted wound, we hurt ourselves by keeping the traditions of men.

Indeed, I want to tell you we cannot be standing on the word of God if we observe men's traditions, and I assure you, any Christian can be guilty of having blind faith, even without knowing they are standing on blind faith. I want you to know that believing a lie, supporting it, and not knowing any better is blind faith.

I assure you, Christians can shout and express their emotions, say long prayers, and sing about what it's like up there. But if they keep the traditions of men, then they make the word of God of no effect, and the excellent Son of God says so.

The definition of vain means not having any real significant value, and vain means worthless, empty, futile, and fruitless. Truly, there's only one way to be certain: we aren't being a part of vain worship and not coasting through Christianity, and the next statement reveals the formula.

Indeed, we'll have to open up our great Bible, read the scriptures, obey them, and avoid the commandments of men. We'll have to distinguish between the clean, unclean, godly, and ungodly, and this is the will of God and His expectation for believers in Christ.

We must try to live by the great Ten Commandments and not keep a counterfeit Sabbath Day. Then, we can be certain we aren't worshipping the great God of Heaven and Earth in vain and aren't being influenced by compromisers to do wrong.

We cannot lay aside God's infallible commandments, pick up men's philosophies, and still please our wonderful Creator God. Truly, we would be unlearned and foolish to believe that the word of man supersedes God's perfect and righteous word.

Mark 7:8 Jesus says, for laying aside the commandments of God, ye hold the traditions of men, as (important as) the washing of pots and cups; and many such things you do.

Indeed, pots and cups need washing regularly, and it's a tradition for men to wash them. But washing pots and cups has no connection to keeping the commanded word of God, nor do the traditions of men have any special connection to the word of God.

Positively, the word of God is extremely special, and the word of God is too special to replace it with counterfeits and accept the made-up traditions of men. The Bible tells us that keeping men's conjured-up traditions makes the word of God of no effect, and the Son of God says so.

Without a doubt, making the word of God of no effect illustrates one of the worst mistakes a Christian can make, and this serious story, *Coasting Through Christianity*, is meant to warn Christians about the perils of making the word of God of no effect.

This story about the strength of our relationship with God is called *Coasting Through Christianity*. It's a revelation story, too, and all Christians should take its message seriously, and coasters should realize there's plenty of work to do for the glory of God.

The analogy of this informative story reveals hot and on-fire Christians are much more preferred than coasting Christians because the hot and on-fire Christian will accomplish much more than a coaster Christian. I must say the joy of the Lord is expressed the best through an exuberant Christian willing to advance the gospel of God.

The commandments of men and the traditions of men may seem good and holy. But they are a smoke screen hiding the truth and aren't an acceptable replacement for the perfect word of God. For this reason, I warn you no philosophy is an acceptable replacement for the original word of God.

Positively, and as a matter of fact, washing pots and cups is way more important than keeping the traditions of men. Indeed, everything we do in opposition to the infallible word of God can kill the effectiveness of the word of God.

Furthermore, I shouldn't need to say or tell any believer in Christ; it's a terrible compromise when we substitute the truth for a lie. Truly, when we substitute the truth for a lie, it takes away the strength of our worship and the closeness of our relationship with Him.

Indeed, we believers in God cannot coast through Christianity, be sleepy watchmen, and have a strong relationship with the God of creation. Furthermore, it could be possible our prize of immortality is in jeopardy if we prefer to coast through Christianity.

Therefore, if I were you, I would take the advice of Jesus Christ and not lay aside the righteous commandments of God and then favor the traditions of men. Because it's vain and naive to believe the All-Mighty God of Heaven and Earth doesn't require professing Christians to know His required word and perfect Ten Commandments.

This truth means coasting through Christianity; being a sleepy Christian is much like being a lukewarm Christian. And coasting through Christianity isn't a God-inspired characteristic, nor should it be one of our characteristics.

However, being hopelessly in love, hot, and on fire for the gospel truth is a God-inspired characteristic that parallels well with a Christian personality. Before this story ends, I must say that even a dumb ox will obey his master better than some Christians will obey God.

This teaching story, I am calling Coasting Through Christianity, profiles passive and lukewarm Christians as coasters. I am warning all coasters: the life-saving word of God should be loved immensely, meditated on daily, and expressed through our decision-making.

The beautiful word of God is a raging fire, and a devout God lover cannot contain it, so standing in the fire and soaking up the heat is their heart's desire. However, coasting through Christianity, Christians need a winter coat to warm them on a hot day.

CHAPTER TWELVE

TWO SIDES OF THE COIN

As the old saying goes, there are two sides to every coin, and this analogy is true, but only one side is good, and the other is wicked. However, I must tell you that this explanation story isn't about any coins. Still, this explanation story is about two opposing sides at war with each other, and both sides have different philosophies on life.

The word coin in this story is a paraphrase, and a paraphrase is a rewording of the meaning of something spoken or written. The subjects in this story are opposing characteristics and opposing forces, whether natural or unnatural in origin.

Truly, if you paraphrase both sides of the coin, make any sense of what I am saying, and be able to relate to my analogy. Then, you'll have to believe two invisible supernatural forces living on the Earth oppose each other in the same way, positive and negative, oppose each other.

Furthermore, because this world has more creations than us roaming the Earth, one supernatural force among us is positive, and the other is negative, and to add to the glamor of these opposing forces, who have supernatural powers beyond our understanding.

It appears for certain both of them have compelling abilities we flesh and blood men and women cannot always overcome. But we must resist the forces of evil because they have an evil agenda to destroy and will not leave us alone or decide not to bother us.

Mainly because bothering us is something they enjoy doing, and it gives them an overwhelming pleasure to trouble us and influence us to do wickedly. We are being challenged every day we live and breathe to defeat them in a game, and the goal of their game is to pull us away from God.

However, regardless of their game, Christians are commanded by God to overcome the forces of evil and not fall prey to their temptations. I want you to realize overcoming the forces of evil can be accomplished by obeying the righteous Ten Commandments of God.

Mainly because the exceedingly special Ten Commandments of God are a game changer, and they are our excellent Instruction manual. Thanks to our Great Creator God, the commandments of God tell us how to avoid and resist the temptations of evil.

However, we have another great source of help, and thanks to God, it's an invisible and righteous compelling force. He purposely speaks the righteousness of God to our hearts, and He understands the evil game spirits play with our everyday lives.

He's called the wonderful Holy Ghost and warns our spirit when our character is pulled away from God's Ten Commandments. If we love righteousness, the moral force of the Holy Ghost is our friend, and we believers in Christ can depend on His excellent guidance.

He'll never leave or forsake us unless we harden our hearts toward Him and refuse to listen to His voice. If we make this mistake, He'll swiftly part company with us. The flip side of the coin means we'll have to love Him and listen to Him if we want to keep Him as our friend.

Again, we need to paraphrase both sides of the coin scenario and entwine our lives to paraphrase. As each day passes, the events of our lives can land on either side of the coin. I must say, with one hundred percent certainty, the spirits of the air try hard to influence us.

Therefore, I warn you, we better stay on guard and constantly guard our hearts and thoughts. Otherwise, we'll listen to the bad spirits, and the compelling evil forces of the air will pull us away from righteousness, and we'll start doing the wrong things.

Furthermore, if you take notice and properly evaluate the horrors of this world, then you'll be forced to realize that the forces of evil are behind all the horrors happening among us. In your evaluation, I am sure your analogy will conclude the spirits of demons are numerous and extremely overwhelming.

All evidence of horrors points to Lucifer as the dominant and barbaric center of strength for the compelling forces of evil. I am sure the ability to murder innocent people comes from the depths of a hardened heart, molded and shaped by the Serpent of Old.

Furthermore, responsibility for the ongoing wars in this middle place between Heaven and Hell and good and evil have a root source, and the forces of evil fuel the wars. Undoubtedly, one of many reasons for war is that the forces of evil put no value on another person's life.

I am certain the condition of this world can change quickly, and good and peaceful people will cease to exist when evil rules this planet. I know the people who believe in God would be erased from this Earth if they didn't stand strong and defend themselves against the forces of evil.

I assure you any person would have to think and operate outside the law of the Ten Commandments to ally with the forces of evil, mainly because the ability to do evil cannot be found in men and women who are determined to live by the Ten Commandments of God.

God's perfect and wonderful word reveals a fact of life, and I am telling you, there are two kinds of seed living on this Earth. The seeds planted in the Garden of God are as opposite as a two-sided coin: one seed is the wheat, and the other is the ungodly tares.

Positively, the two opposing seeds are revealed in the New Testament. The wonderful Son of God explains them to us in the book of Matthew, chapter thirteen, verses thirty-seven and thirty-eight. Furthermore, I want you to realize the charming and wicked Lucifer introduced the bad seed to this world, and they are here to choke out the wheat.

Evidence starts at the beginning of the angel rebellion in Heaven and during the first Earth age, before the great cleansing flood. Evidence proves the wicked Lucifer and his seed are the forces of evil, and we would be foolish to drift away from God and play on their side of the field.

However, on the other side of the coin, called the positive side, because of God's formula, life's characteristics are much better. Evidence proves the children of God are recognized by their characteristics of godliness, peace, harmony, and love for each other.

History proves evil forces establish their image through a conquering brutal force determined to murder and destroy all opposition to them. As always, greed and envious rebellion against godliness, righteousness, and opposition to peace motivate evil forces to kill, steal, and destroy.

Indeed, the angelic author, my God, chose to be cast out of Heaven and guilty of putting a definition to the word and emotion of evil. It's the wicked Lucifer, the Serpent of Old, the glittering charming star. And because of wickedness, God has exiled him from His kingdom of Utopia.

It's amazing how the forces of evil and righteousness co-existed down the corridors of time. Especially considering their incompatibility and the compelling power and control Lucifer has over the hearts and thoughts of weak and ungodly men, not subject to the commandments of God.

I guarantee the history of this unstable world proves evil works and evil emotions are the real reason righteous men and women do self-defense. This truth means evil works are the trigger, activating self-defense from the forces of righteousness.

Evil works, combined with the tangible and intangible forces of evil, are the complete formula for wars and troubles among all men throughout every generation. I conclude that if weak-minded men and women weren't puppets doing the will of the wicked puppet master, then the formula for evil could be defeated.

Anyway, I assure you, the forces of evil and the terrible characteristics of rebellion are staunch allies, and both have the same ungodly goal they try hard to achieve. Because believers in God and the tares have different goals, the war between good and evil will not end until the Son of God returns as a reaper from Heaven.

Indeed, I am certain that evil-doers' ungodly characteristics are usually the same, and the word of God doesn't hinder them. It's regardless of whether they are flesh and blood evildoers or the wicked, rebellious demonic spirits of the air evil doers.

It's always their goal to pull all men and women away from the righteous word of God and not allow the word of God to grow strong among the forces of evil. As we can see with our own eyes, we can make observations based on the world's general condition.

The uncompassionate forces of evil will not rest until the perfect Ten Commandments and God's infallible and righteous ways are meaningless to mankind. Since the rebellious Lucifer set his feet upon this Earth, it's been his goal to destroy the wonderful word of God.

Positively, it's easy to see that the excellent word of God is meaningless to most of this world. It's especially easy to see if we care enough to evaluate the moral condition of society. After an evaluation, we'll realize who is shaping the condition of society the most.

Indeed, uncleanness, ungodliness, and unrighteousness are the immoral standards of the forces of evil, and all these ungodly characteristics have a root connection to Lucifer. I want you to know Lucifer is the evil tree mentioned in the book of Genesis disguised as a snake in the Garden of God.

Positively, the god of evil is the satanic Lucifer, and he warred against the God of creation in Heaven. Undoubtedly, the war he caused was vicious and brutal, and maybe we were involved in it, too, since we lived in Heaven during our beginning.

Indeed, the wicked Lucifer is the god of evil, and his character never improves, and he's opposed to peace on Earth. Truly, even a blind man suffering from a physical impairment should be able to understand the source behind evil.

Written within the book of Revelation, we are warned by the scripture saying, an angel comes down from Heaven to release evil upon this Earth. When he descends from Heaven, the angel will have the keys to the bottomless pit, the prison of Hell.

The angel will release the physical bodies of demons upon this Earth and leave the gates of Hell open for an unknown amount of time. After their release day, near the end of this second Earth age, the Earth will become as it was before the great cleansing flood.

I am certain the conditions of this Earth will worsen for everyone, and it'll be slaughter time all over again, caused by the ruthless forces of evil, who lack the emotion of love. They'll direct their violence toward anyone, not with the seal of God on their forehead.

Without a doubt, when they are released from the bottomless pit, the demons from Hell will take control of the whole Earth. But their control will be temporary, and they'll lose it when the Son of God returns with a sharp sword protruding from His mouth.

Furthermore, when He does return, this explanation story I am calling two sides of the coin. It'll turn into a story concerning one side of the coin because the wonderful Son of God will remove the forces of evil from the Earth, and He'll do it by force.

After that, the Earth will make a wonderful transformation, and there will only be God lovers and lovers of righteousness left to live on the Earth. For our benefit and the glory of God, the Son of God will be the new King forever and ever.

Praise the Lord!

CHAPTER THIRTEEN

SANCTIFIED AND PURE

This revealing story, as important as any other subject written in the Bible, is *Sanctified And Pure*. It's meant to illuminate an extremely personal day, and this personal day means a great deal to the God of Heaven and Earth, and it's called the Lord's Day.

The Lord's Day is special to Him and was chosen and set aside by Him, and it's different from the other six days of the week. His blessed and hallowed personal day means more to Him than to most professing Christians, and if we do right, we'll illustrate honor to Him by keeping His set apart day.

Furthermore, most believers in Christ care nothing about His extremely personal day, and some do not recognize it or endeavor to treat it as special. However, they want to be divinely blessed and cared for by Him and hope He'll not penalize them for breaking His Sabbath.

Positively, I am certain all Christians want God to bless them with prosperity and watch over them, and this is a fair request to expect if we are loyal Christians in love with His word and are devout commandment keepers. I know most Christians are steadfast and keep nine of His commandments.

I know for certain it must seem grievous, hard to accept, and hard for some Christians to commit themselves to the fourth commandment of God. However, a patterned ritual proves the fourth commandment is unacceptable to most Christians.

Indeed, the fact is clear and for the benefit of obedience to our wonderful God. We should do as our Great Creator God asks us to and keep the sacred seventh day holy and separate from the other six days of the week.

Furthermore, if you are a professing Christian, the original word of God should also be extremely important to you. Truly, all professing Christians should desire and love to keep the authentic word of God, and they should delight in doing His will.

The next informative scripture is the absolute word of God, and our Great Creator God speaks it, and it's also the unchangeable fourth commandment of God. I want you to know His fourth commandment is as valid as the other nine, and we are foolish to debate the word of God.

> **Deuteronomy 5:14** But the <u>seventh day</u> (Saturday) is the <u>Sabbath</u> (the holy, sacred, and blessed day) of the Lord thy God.

The next revealing scripture is the commanded word of God, and God speaks it. Bible scriptures reveal our Great Creator God commands *sanctification* (cleanness) for His seventh-day Sabbath Day, and He's not kidding around.

I want you to know that sanctify means free from sin, holy, set apart, sacred, clean, special, hallowed, and completely kept clean. Again, I am telling you, my Great God isn't kidding around, and He uses the word keep and sanctify because He wants obedience.

> **Deuteronomy 5:12** and God says, keep the <u>Sabbath Day</u> (the seventh day Sabbath Day) to *sanctify* (means to keep it holy and clean,

Deuteronomy 5:12 sets it apart from the other six days (including Sunday) as the Lord thy God commands thee.

Indeed, according to the unchangeable word of God, and spoken by God, Sun-day is another work day of the week and not special at all. The scriptures prove that Sun-day is the first day of the week, and it's not holy or set apart, and God does not sanctify it.

I know it's the nature of most professing Christian men and women to do their own thing. I believe because it's a way of life for the whole world, the Sunday Christians want to prosper on the seventh day of the week, as the unbelievers do.

However, I want you to know that you shouldn't have to be told; the unbelievers have a completely different mindset concerning right and wrong. The holy things considered special to our wonderful God aren't special to the unbelievers.

This truth means it's unimportant for the unbeliever to reverence our Great Creator God. Unbelievers will not set one minute apart and treat His Sabbath Day special to illustrate their love for Him. Sadly, loyal believers in Christ are disadvantaged in Sabbath Day recognition because the world doesn't recognize the fourth commandment.

I believe professing Christians mean no harm when they defile and break the holy and sacred fourth commandment. But the fact remains clear: We live by the ways of man or the ways of God, and the gift of free will allows us to make our own choices.

Beyond the shadow of a doubt, if there's a choice between man's and our Great God's ways, it would be much better for Christians to obey God's rather than man's. I want you to realize this existence is a life and death test, and passing the test depends on you and me living by His word.

Because we cannot be sanctified and pure if we forfeit the ways of our Great God and choose to live by man's ways, there's no logical reason, reward, or divine blessings from the God of Heaven and Earth for keeping man's ways. Truly, I advise you to live Christ-like and keep the commandments of God.

Indeed, there are absolute promises and great rewards we cannot imagine for keeping the ways of our Great Creator God. But for some illogical reason, most men and women will let the pleasures of sin or the traditions of men keep them from being sanctified.

Surely, when we discover the definition of sanctify, we will set ourselves apart from ungodliness and uncleanness. Then our eyes will open, and we'll realize that the word sanctify is a perfect description of the character of God in many ways, and we better try to emulate His character.

I'll repeat the definition of the word sanctify, and you can make your comparison to the word sanctify and to the character of God. Although the definition of sanctify cannot fully compare to the character of God, it does have good similarities.

The word sanctify means hallowed, holy, sacred, free from sin, set apart from ungodliness, clean, and extremely special. Now, I'll ask you, doesn't the word sanctified describe the character and the image of our extremely Special God and His character examples we should adapt to our character?

For us believers in Him, the word sanctify means we should respect what is holy and sacred to God because He's holy and sacred and free from sin. His word is holy and sacred, and we should try extremely hard to be like Him and emulate His righteous and beautiful character.

For us believers in Him, the word pure means you and me, and everyone else, should hate all sorts of sin. It's because our great and righteous Creator God hates all sin, and it's a violation of the covenant to sin. For your protection, conform to the great Ten Commandments of God because they are designed to prevent sin.

In the book of Deuteronomy, God tells us to sanctify the seventh day, Sabbath Day, and to keep it holy. Because of parallels, it's easy to conclude the seventh day, Sabbath Day, and the perfect character of God are both entwined to the word sanctify.

This truth means God's wonderful and perfect character and the word sanctify are similar in definition and entwine better than a scrub brush and soap. Surely, there isn't anything more holy than the character of God and the definition of sanctifying and pure.

This truth is because our wonderful and Great God is the Holy of holies, and I guarantee you that no flesh and blood person or angel is as holy as Him. We cannot be as holy as Him, but God requires us to <u>sanctify, setting</u> ourselves apart from commandment breaking.

Furthermore, my Great God never changes His expectations throughout every generation before and after us. After thousands of years, the formula for being set apart is still the same today as it's always been during the previous years.

God searches the heart and the soul of every man and woman on this Earth, regardless of the nation's name. In His search throughout the Earth, He's looking for separated people who abhor the unholy, as He abhors everything ungodly.

Beyond the shadow of a doubt, my all-mighty God is looking for people to call His own who are in love with His righteous ways. He's looking for special people who wish to be sanctified and pure, as He, His Son, and the Holy Ghost are sanctified.

Therefore, since the seventh day, Sabbath Day is sanctified and pure, nearly the same way His name and character are sanctified, then He's saying, respect and care about the seventh day, Sabbath Day, in the same manner as we respect our Holy God.

Within the next meaningful to God scripture, our wonderful God pours out His heart and makes known His greatest desire. Indeed, His greatest desire entwines with the definition of sanctification and our determination and ability to rise above sin.

> **Deuteronomy 5:29** O' that there is such a heart in <u>them</u> (meaning the children of Israel, and the Christians who love Him), that they would <u>fear</u> (means reverence) Me,

> **Deuteronomy 5:29** and <u>keep</u> (means obey and delight in) <u>all</u> (means every one of) My commandments always, that it might be well with them and their children forever!

The great God-Bible assures us of reverence to God, and keeping the righteous Ten Commandments is the whole duty of man. Furthermore, not forgetting to keep the fourth commandment illustrates a part of our reverence for our wonderful God.

Our Supreme Lord says all will go well with our children and us forever if we revere Him and keep His commandments. I assure you God isn't asking us to do something hard, and we should be glad to be faithful commandment keepers.

I want you to know there are not many promises from our wonderful God as rewarding and protective as knowing God watches over us. He tells us life will go well with our children and us forever if we revere Him, keep His commandments, and sanctify the seventh day, Sabbath Day.

Therefore, if we diligently teach the Ten Commandments to our children, regard them high above the traditions of men, remember their importance, keep them close to our hearts, and write them on the doorposts of our houses and gates.

Then we'll always be extremely special people unto our great God, and He'll remember us when He's passing out the keys to Heaven. Also, remember, when our spirit leaves the flesh, we will want the keys to Heaven.

This personal to God story, *Sanctified And Pure*, describes all His friends in Heaven. I hope to see you there in a white robe, sanctified and pure, and drinking pure water as it flows from the throne of God.

I am sure being set apart from sin is the destiny our Great Creator God desires for you and me, and when our destiny entwines with His desires, we'll be sanctified and pure. Indeed, because we are faithful, love Him, and walk in His ways, you and I will receive a white robe when we enter His kingdom.

CHAPTER FOURTEEN

REVENGE

This concerning story, I am calling revenge, portrays an image all of us might relate to at some time or another during our lives. However, I must say that revenge isn't a good character quality because we must go against God's word to seek revenge.

Revenge and hate go hand in hand, most of the time, and seeking revenge means someone wants to punish someone else in return for something the person did to them in the past. Usually, our natural impulse is to retaliate against whoever hurts us.

Indeed, our emotions rule our hearts to a major degree, and sometimes, men and women seek revenge and retaliation. Retaliation is a form of getting even with someone, regardless of the commanded word of God, and this is man's way.

However, where does revenge stop, and is revenge a righteous reaction to everything someone does to us? God assures us that revenge is not a righteous reaction from us, even though this analogy is hard to accept when someone has wronged us.

However, Bible scriptures reveal all revenge belongs to our wonderful Creator God, and the next absolute scripture tells us revenge belongs to Him. Surely, if we trust in Him, we'll allow Him to do what's necessary.

Deuteronomy 32:35 To <u>Me</u> (God) belongeth vengeance, and recompense:

The definition of compensation (discipline) means something given or done through retaliation in return for a wrong. Vengeance and recompense are the way reactions are determined for punishment, and I want you to know nothing escapes the all-seeing eyes of God.

This truth means our Great Supernatural God is watching from above and is a fair compensation God, and the laws of God, man, and penalties are enforced through some vengeance or recompense. However, the righteous laws of my great God are the highest pinnacle of the law since they have a say in the judgment of damnation.

I hope you realize that our Great God has many means of applying recompense to wicked men, and it could be possible the need for compensation began in Heaven with our Most High God. Undoubtedly, the works performed by Lucifer in the kingdom of God prove recompense was needed as a form of disciplinary action.

Beyond the shadow of a doubt, acts of vengeance and hate are the two main reasons the wicked Lucifer wanted the wonderful Son of God murdered. I am certain the wicked Lucifer didn't want Yeshua to rise from the grave three days after His death and prove His power of resurrection.

The two main reasons for killing the wonderful Son of God were revenge for being cast out of Heaven and the other reason is extreme hate because he couldn't be the Highest God. Undoubtedly, these two reasons reveal the character of Lucifer as wicked, rebellious, and evil.

Indeed, the wicked Lucifer didn't have feelings of love, and he hated God terribly because he couldn't permanently redesign the bloodline of

Adam and Eve and make it into his race of mixed-bloodline people to worship him. But Satan tried and failed, and he will burn in the lake of fire.

Furthermore, the terrible and vengeful death Lucifer planned for the Son of God during the time of King Herod. It was revenge for his failures and woes in Heaven, during the first Earth age, before the great flood, and because Yeshua wouldn't bow down and worship him.

Anyway, I want you to know that my Great all-mighty God of Heaven and Earth is supernatural and capable of administering recompense. Gloriously, my Supernatural God says revenge belongs to Him, and He will collect all sinful debts until they are paid in full.

Furthermore, Bible scriptures reveal revenge did belong to God when He was angered before the great flood. Gloriously, my wonderful God of judgment sent the cleansing flood because Lucifer mixed his bloodline with the flesh and created a third bloodline.

However, even after the great cleansing flood, the wicked spirit of Lucifer is a dangerous adversary of humankind. I want you to know Satan has many servants of sin, but many of them live in the flesh, and the righteous word of God doesn't bind them.

The charming Lucifer isn't physical anymore and hasn't got an army of angelic physical servants anymore. But his new flesh and blood servants of sin are the rebellious instruments he uses to keep hate alive and do his revenge on the children of God.

Even though hate and revenge began with heavenly creations after they rebelled against the God of creation, there's been an enormous overspill of revenge since then, and it includes nearly every human being on this Earth. Sometimes, even the children who love God submit to His influence when they open Pandora's box, especially the ones who eat the unclean.

Indeed, you and I would be rebelling against our Great God if we took revenge into our own hands. Truly, I know not doing personal revenge is one of the reasons for His laws, and my Great God sitting on the throne in Heaven is the Great Judge.

Positively, personal revenge from us isn't pleasing to God, although self-defense is acceptable, and self-defense is needed sometimes. However, if you and I want to be pleasing to God, we must resist hate, revenge, and personal compensation.

This truth means that if we believe in God and the truthfulness of His word, we shouldn't seek personal revenge because revenge belongs to Him. But please do not confuse revenge with justice because penalizing lawless men for injustices is right.

The next informative scripture says, do not avenge ourselves, but leave recompense to God. Our Great God is watching from above, and I am certain He orchestrates vengeance sometimes, and we do not realize it. But be assured God will repay evil and wicked people appropriately.

Romans 12:19 Dearly beloved, avenge not yourselves, but rather <u>give place</u> <u>unto</u> wrath (means do not take personal revenge):

Romans 12:19 For it is written, <u>vengeance</u> (means recompense) is <u>Mine</u> (means God's); <u>I</u> (God) will repay saith the Lord.

If we are compassionate Christians, have love in our hearts for everyone, and want to live peacefully among all men. Then, taking matters into our hands and seeking personal vengeance and recompense isn't right for us.

Please do not be naïve enough to believe evil men will not exploit us, especially if we have kind and soft hearts. Please do not let misguided love be the reason; we live unguarded against the corrupt forces of evil.

I assure you, it would be blind faith to live an unguarded life in this wicked world, and positively, an ounce of prevention is worth a pound of cure. I am certain we can avoid many unsavory circumstances if we listen to the voice of the Holy Ghost.

However, do not give place to wrath, and do not take personal vengeance into your own hands if it's possible to avoid it. Our Father in Heaven, the God of Christians, will repay our enemies with His perfect recompense.

I am quite certain hate, and personal revenge isn't a tool for Christians to use, but putting the wrong done to you in the hands of God is the right thing to do. Indeed, state policemen and deputy sheriffs have a job to do, and the courts discipline lawbreakers, too.

However, vengeance belongs to the Lord, not us, and He wouldn't say so if it weren't true. Furthermore, it's a scary moment when anyone falls into the wrathful hands of the Lord, and criminals may avoid the law sometimes, but they cannot avoid the all-seeing eyes of God.

I am certain hate and revenge were established upon this Earth after Lucifer was cast onto it, and hate and revenge will be removed from this Earth when Lucifer and his ungodly children are removed from among the wheat.

This truth means the terrible emotion of hate and revenge follows in the footsteps of the wicked and rebellious Lucifer since he encourages hate and revenge. Please realize before the Son of God returns to destroy the tares, this world will wax worse and worse.

Indeed, it'll be glorious when hate and revenge are replaced with love, peace, and harmony. But the expected glorious day of peace and harmony hasn't arrived yet. However, the glorious day will arrive when the Son of God returns to cleanse the Earth, and the wrath of the reapers will not spare wicked men.

However, please be aware Christians may be able to keep themselves in check, but most of this world is out of check. This truth means this world is motivated to a large degree by hate and revenge, and it's the main reason for compensation.

Conclusively, self-defense isn't the same as revenge and hate, and self-defense is necessary for this life. Truly, do not be reluctant to defend yourself, your family, or anyone in need. Be similar to Moses and Joshua, and do not hesitate to fight against evil men.

I assure you Christians aren't expected to be similar to helpless rabbits, and God does expect us to do self-defense, not needless revenge. But this world is full of lawbreakers and evil men, and when they do wickedly. If possible, we should let the law deal with them.

CHAPTER FIFTEEN

SERVING GOD FOR PROFIT

Whether we approve or disapprove, profit and prosperity are on everyone's mind, regardless of whether we believe in the Son of God or are a servant of Satan. We all know keeping food on the table and a roof over our heads takes a certain amount of prosperity.

Maybe the only difference between the two types of profit seekers is how they earn their profits. We all know profit-seeking is the American way, and it's the way of everyone else in most other countries to be a profit seeker.

All the above being said, in defense of profit seekers, I have to say there's a red line profit seekers shouldn't cross, and I want you to know the red line is much more restricted for loyal men of God than the red line is for the unbelievers.

However, when there's no moral boundary line to cross, it gives the unbelievers an advantage in seeking profits. But this informative story isn't for the unbelievers' benefit; it's written for whoever believes in Christ.

Furthermore, this enlightenment story mostly focuses on insincere and corrupt men in the pulpit. However, if this story identifies with you, me, or anyone else, then so be it because compatibilities are compatibilities.

Most unbelievers could care less about how they seek and secure their profits, and because of their disconnect from my wonderful God, they aren't concerned about having an effective prayer line with our Creator God.

However, it's much different with Christians, and it's logical to assume that every church and every Christian wants their place of worship to be pure and effective. All Christians want an effective worship center where their prayers will be listened to and considered by our Great God.

Because vain worship and vain prayers are a waste of time and effort, I am an example Christian, and I do not want to do anything to make my prayers of no effect between God and me. For this reason, I assure you that doing ungodly things will lessen our odds of getting answered prayers.

Truly, I want you to know that it would be devastating for me and other Christians to believe the excellent and wonderful word of God was made of no effect in our lives because of the traditions of men. According to the scriptures, replacing the word of God with the traditions of men will cause God to close His ears to our prayers.

Throughout this extremely serious story, I'll reveal some things that cause the word of God to be of no effect. Sadly, the life of a professing Christian that's not effective daily bears no fruit, and no fruit equals a waste of time.

Although the life of an effective Christian will bear much fruit and multiply many times over, his efforts will be effective. Truly, it's logical to assume a true and genuine Christian will want to bear much fruit and do many good works for the glory of God.

Mainly because it's natural for Christians to want well for each other, and it pleases God to see us care for someone in need. All Christians want well for one another if they truly care about their brothers and sisters in Christ, and our conscience is numb to compassion if we do not.

An authentic Christian loves to see the wonderful word of God multiply and spread around like the sands of the sea. But I want you to know that whenever God's wonderful gospel is taught, it must be taught authentically.

Indeed, we must prove ourselves Christ-like before effectiveness can be achieved and results manifest through prayer. Whenever we make a prayer request, the effectiveness of our prayer can be attributed to the inspiration of the Holy Ghost; who knows if we are conforming to the word of God?

Truly, the Holy Ghost of God has requirements, and obedience to His requirements will improve effectiveness. Anything less than obedience to His requirements will destroy effectiveness and the inspiration intended for us to receive from the Holy Ghost.

Indeed, the preacher preaching behind the pulpit can increase or destroy effectiveness. For this reason, do not be charmed by smiling snakes in the pulpit, planning and scheming for profit. Furthermore, we are a fool not to realize the collection plate is snake food for corrupt preachers.

Mainly because there are many wolves in sheep's clothing in the Sunday churches, and they are disguised in the best of clothing. But inwardly, they are ravening wolves in sheep's clothing, and they aren't bothered by paganism and the traditions of men.

Furthermore, these ravening wolves are preachers and teachers of false doctrines, and they substitute the wonderful word of God to favor the traditions of men. Sadly, they honor the God of Heaven and Earth with their lips, but their heart doesn't love Him.

They do not care if the excellent word of God and your prize of immortality are hindered within the walls of the Sun-day churches. Nor do they care if the needed word of God is ineffective in the lives of the people they call brother and sister.

Therefore, wolves in sheep's clothing do not care if the prayers of professing Christians are answered or not answered. So, you'll know a ravening wolf in sheep's clothing usually is behind the pulpit, and he's preaching whatever sermon it takes to tickle the ears of Christians.

Mainly because wolves in sheep's clothing and false prophets serve God for profit, and they make a science out of profit sermons. In all reality, the wolves in sheep's clothing do not care if Christians in their Sun-day churches receive divine blessings or nothing from God.

This truth means they do not care if the congregation, who puts their money on the collection plate, receives healing and good fortune from God. But they are extremely happy as long as they can prosper from the congregation's wallet.

Furthermore, just because someone goes to a Sun-day church or even plays gospel music in a Sun-day church doesn't mean it automatically makes them devout Christians who believe in keeping the whole word of God.

It only means they have the appearance of a Christian, and the appearance works because they frequent the church building on Sunday mornings. But pretty words and appearances can be deceiving; in most cases, they are deceiving, especially if they are an insincere projection.

For example, Lucifer's most deceiving appearance is as an angel of light, but our God-inspired Bible doesn't portray him as an angel of light. However, I want you to realize it's correct to say the wolves in sheep's clothing emulate Lucifer, and it's because they appear godly and pure on the outside.

However, inside, Lucifer and the wolves in sheep's clothing, who disguise themselves as persons of the light, aren't light bearers. But the darkness of the heart and darkness of the mind describes them the best, and the light they project is artificial.

Conclusively, make-believe Christians, false prophets, and whoever deceives with false lips, including preachers teaching other than our Great God's righteous gospel, are similar to ravening wolves.

I assure you, insincere words, false faces, and scheming plans are an art of deception, and the art of deception is a runaway train in this world and its missing brakes. For this reason, we better be Bible-savvy to know the truth from a lie or a false appearance will deceive us.

I am certain that the art of deception is the number one ploy and trick that most people on this Earth practice today, and sadly, to say, there's more artificial light in this world than there is pure light. For this reason, I warn you God expects us to know the difference between artificial and pure light.

This truth means we cannot take anyone for face value anymore, not even a large majority of preacher men found behind the pulpit. It's because religious deception is so rampant and commonly practiced it's killed our ability to have faith in most people, including preacher men too.

Furthermore, every preacher behind the pulpit may seem concerned about our salvation and well-being. But inwardly deceiving preachers are only concerned about our wallet giving to their wallet.

Especially if almost everything they preach hinges on tithing, an important factor to the wolves in sheep's clothing. I am certain tithing isn't the number one God-inspired requirement for receiving blessings and salvation.

Furthermore, too much stern emphasis on tithing and a passive grace analogy concerning God's exact word indicates that they serve God for profit. As much as I hate to say so, Lucifer has a great army of wolves in sheep's clothing serving him that deceive for the love of money.

Conclusively, miracles from Heaven do not cost us one penny, and giving a million dollars to a preacher will not cure a toothache, a headache, or a small scratch on the finger. Furthermore, I assure you, no amount of money will buy us passage through the pearl gates.

CHAPTER SIXTEEN

PARABLE OF THE GAME BIRD

Indeed, this is a metaphoric, completely serious, meaningful story and an eye-opener relating to millions of people. This enlightenment story isn't about turkeys or grouse, chickens or ducks, or any animal with feathers. It's not about a game bird; hunters who hunt for sport or food.

Within this enlightenment story, a game bird and its eggs illustrate the right and wrong ways to get rich, and Bible scriptures reveal the right way is by the sweat of our brow. As you already know, because of many examples of the character of men, there are two ways to become rich.

The sweat of the brow phrase is another way of saying The honest way, which is accomplished through fairness. The other way is called ill-gotten gains; gained the wrong way and the wrong way is dishonest, and the hidden character of a man is illustrated when money is involved.

The next informative scripture illustrates the right and wrong ways, and an uncompassionate game bird is used as a metaphor illustration, but we are the parallel game bird. The uncompassionate game bird, not hatching the eggs, sets the standard for paralleling wickedness.

> **Jeremiah 17:11** As the <u>partridge</u> (means the game bird) sitteth on eggs, and hatcheth them not; so (is) he that getteth rich,

> **Jeremiah 17:11** and not by <u>right</u> (means not righteously), shall leave <u>them</u> (the ways of righteousness, and) amid his days, and at his <u>end</u> (at the end of his life he) shall be a fool.

The partridge, the game bird, lays her eggs and hatches them not. She's compared to the rich man, not bound by the word of God, and getting his riches the wrong way. The above scripture says the rich fool getting his riches the wrong way shall be counted as a fool at the end of his life.

Sadly, money consumes the thoughts of some men, and fools who leave the right way and do the wrong things to gain riches during their lives are foolish. However, most of us would be lying if we said we wouldn't want to be rich and not have to worry about our wants and needs.

Indeed, gaining riches through lying and scheming is wrong; every man will be held accountable for their dishonesty. In the same way, the uncompassionate hen abandons her nest, doesn't hatch her eggs, and robs her children of life.

The next declaration scripture concerning the works of our hands reveals the result for men who lie and scheme to gain riches the dishonest way. I want you to know gaining prosperity against the righteous word of God is dishonest, and the corrupt man is a fool to put money before righteousness.

> **Proverbs 14:12** There is a <u>way</u> (the way of the world) which seemeth right unto a man, but the end thereof are the ways of death.

Corrupt men can twist the thoughts in their minds and justify almost anything they do to obtain riches and material gain, regardless if it's done the wrong way. But the corrupt ways of this world and the ungodly ways of men are not the ways of God.

Therefore, when the truth boils down, our Great Creator God makes the rules concerning right and wrong, and you and I do not have a choice concerning the definition of right and wrong. However, we can review the Ten Commandments, know right and wrong, and understand God's expectations.

Living by the Ten Commandments is a requirement if we want to win the prize of immortality, and the wonderful gift of immortality has to be won by observing the rules of God. Indeed, it's His rules and commandments that all men and women will be judged by someday.

Therefore, I am telling you activities that seem right to a man better parallel God's laws and commandments. Otherwise, what seems right to a man will be considered foolish and unacceptable to my Great God. I want you to know repentance and lifestyle change erase many sins, but God doesn't bend His commandments for anyone, and we will be held liable for our ungodliness.

The highway of the upright is to depart from evil, but the highway to Hell is the road traveled by the wicked. Both roads are available; we better choose the right way as we live in the flesh.

I wish we had wisdom in our youth and all our choices were godly. But sadly, to say, we have to learn a lot of things as we grow into a man. So, I advise you to let the Ten Commandments be your teacher.

Indeed, the bible clarifies that the way of eternal life is found on the highway of righteousness. But the way of eternal death is found on the highway of the unrighteous, and I assure you, Lucifer's telepathic influence causes a landslide of unrighteous decisions.

Beyond the shadow of a doubt, the soul of every person is preserved or destroyed, and it depends on the highway we travel. This statement is a true realization that needs to be realized by everyone. However, regardless of the fog on the road, I want you to know we can repent, change, and walk on the right highway.

I assure you, there are no barriers to stopping anyone from traveling on the road of life or the highway to Hell. This truth means our lifestyle choice guides us into the afterlife, and no other substitutes can prevail against His guiding word.

Truly, many preachers teach prosperity, wealth, and health, and they teach the Son of God wants every Christian to be rich with material treasures. I hope every believer in Christ has a good life on this Earth, good health, and earns a good living.

However, if the wonderful Son of God wanted all Christians to be rich and blessed with abundant worldly possessions, then I am asking you, why did Jesus tell the rich man in the book of Matthew to give his excess to the poor? Truly, I want you to know money isn't everything, and we shouldn't love money.

Yeshua wanted the rich man to care more about treasures in Heaven than on Earth; this is how the story goes between the rich man and the Son of God. A concerned young rich man was blessed to have much material wealth and wanted to secure the prize of immortality. The rich man kneeled before the wonderful Son of God and asked, what shall I do to inherit the gift of eternal life?

The wonderful Son of God said unto the rich man; thou knowest the commandments of God, and most people do. Yeshua says the commandments are the formula for eternal life; the same goes for everyone interested in living in His kingdom forever.

Indeed, the next few important words, the wonderful Son of God, speak to the rich man. They illuminate the requirements for eternal life, and if we were to ask Him, should I take your commandments seriously? Then, I am certain He would say yes.

The wonderful Son of God tells the rich man, do not kill, do not commit adultery, do not steal, do not bear false witness. The wonderful Son of God tells him to defraud no one and honor his father and Mother.

The Ten Commandments are the conclusion to the whole matter, consisting of two hundred and ninety-five simple spoken words, and it's easy to conclude God didn't want them to be complicated or hard to understand. For these reasons, He wrote them in simple words.

The Ten Commandments are our only directions leading to eternal life, and not utilizing them will restrict us from obtaining eternal life. For this reason, the guiding Ten Commandments are the greatest message ever given to the angels and mankind.

The straight-spoken Son of God loved the young rich man, and He wanted the rich man to secure eternal life and live in His kingdom. The caring Son of God told him to sell what he had and give it to the poor, and after that, he would have treasures in Heaven.

However, the young rich man was similar to almost all rich men, and he learned to depend on his riches rather than depend on God. The young rich man was sad because he didn't want to part with his riches and wasn't willing to trust in God completely.

Afterward, Yeshua told His disciples how difficult it is for a rich man to enter the kingdom of Heaven because rich men value their riches the most. Surely, going after ill-gotten gain proves some men are willing to go beyond the boundaries of God to be rich.

The young rich man had the greatest opportunity of his life; all he had to do was listen to Jesus, and the same goes for you and me. I want you to realize he wasn't just offered the gift of salvation in the kingdom of God, but the young rich man was offered much more while living in the flesh.

This truth means he could've walked and traveled with the Son of God from that day forth and become a special part of His ministry. But he turned down the great honor of being a special disciple of the Son of God because he didn't want to part with his riches.

I am certain if the young rich man had given up his riches and followed after Yeshua, the excellent Son of God. Then, he would've inherited a noble position in Heaven and had unimaginable treasures waiting for him in the beautiful kingdom of God.

Many times, in my teaching stories, I've said all the silver and gold in this world cannot buy the prize of immortality, and the gift of immortality is a great prize, and we do have to win it. I want you to know that decision-making will challenge our ability to win the prize of immortality.

Indeed, salvation, eternal life, and supernatural immortality are the same, and securing a home in the Kingdom of God is the prize we win for loving God. I want you to know that loving God has to be proved with more than pretty words, and commandment keeping proves we love the beautiful and perfect God of Heaven and Earth.

Furthermore, I guarantee you that our future habitation place isn't determined by how much material wealth we possess in this life, and the grand prize of immortality must be earned correctly. It cannot be bought with silver and gold or anything of tangible value.

Therefore, the partridge symbolizes the game bird and is not compassionate enough to care about doing right. But the game bird symbolizes the ungodly rich man, who'll lie and deceive for the love of money.

Indeed, this is a metaphor story example, and as the wonderful Son of God separates the sheep from the male goats. I assure you that Yeshua will separate the players from the sincere, righteous, and unrighteous.

Therefore, the game bird, who hatcheth not her eggs, isn't different than the rich man, who puts ungodliness before godliness. Thanks to God we are given the analogy of the uncompassionate game bird, portraying an example of wickedness.

Furthermore, the conclusion of this extremely serious story concerning the game bird and getting riches the right way reveals an uncompassionate person is a fool at the end of their life because God doesn't like the metaphor game bird that will not hatch her eggs.

The next scripture, concerning me and you and our choices in life, will reveal the heart of God and His thoughts and judgment concerning the metaphor game bird. This extremely serious next scripture reveals a price tag attached to uncompassionate acts.

Jeremiah 17:10 I the Lord search the heart, I <u>try</u> (means I test) <u>the reigns</u> (means the heart), even to <u>give</u> (means repay,) every man according to his ways, and according to the fruit of his doings.

Indeed, this meaningful metaphor story God shares about the game bird is also a warning story, and the warning in this story means that God is watching us and evaluating our works, and He will repay accordingly.

Therefore, this important metaphor warning story should be absorbed into our hearts and taken extremely seriously, mainly because my Great God wrote the metaphor game bird story with a pen of iron. His pen of iron has the point of a diamond, and everything He writes is permanent.

For the above reason, we need to understand the game bird story. Its definition and meaning will never change, and the corridors of time will parallel many men and women to the uncompassionate game bird. I want you to know the wicked Lucifer parallels the uncompassionate game bird and he's a killer of life and not a preserver.

Furthermore, this story about the game bird laying eggs and hatching them not expands to include other serious matters in this world. The next scripture reveals a fitting end to this teaching story, the game bird, and it brings God's analogy to a close.

Jeremiah 17:5 Thus saith the Lord; Cursed be the man that trusteth in man, and maketh flesh his arm, and whose heart departeth from the Lord.

Conclusively, a heart departed from the Lord parallels the cursed person to the game bird, who refuses to do right. If the definition of a fool could expand to include one more thing, it would include everyone refusing to do right.

CHAPTER SEVENTEEN

SHORTENED TO FIVE MONTHS

This revealing story, *Shortened To Five Months*, is about the end of time and the tribulation on this Earth being entwined with killer creatures from Hell. This end-time story parallels the Bible and reveals an urgent necessity to bring back the Son of God sooner than anticipated and much less than seven years.

I want you to know that the Earth's great prophesized tribulation time is unusual, and because of design, it will come true. This story coincides with a specific time after the wicked Lucifer and the other rebellious angels are released from the pits of Hell.

Furthermore, the great tribulation time, entwined with supernatural creatures, was intended to last seven years. But escalated end-time events will urgently require the return of Yeshua sooner than seven years. Prophecy reveals that believers in Christ will pray for His second return, and we should be daily.

Positively, for the *elect's sake*, God will shorten the last three and one-half years of the tribulation time to five months. This truth means His elect people, alias believers in Him, are still here during the great tribulation time and haven't been raptured.

Beyond the shadow of a doubt, when these next two revealing scriptures are combined. They reveal a troubling time and insinuate a need to shorten the tribulation time. I want you to know the wicked Lucifer and the murderous, rebellious angels are the reason the tribulation time needs to be shortened.

However, I am certain it'll not be shortened for the benefit of the unbelievers. But our wonderful and Great God looks out for His loyal children, and the tribulation time will be shortened for the *elect's sake*. The *elect* are whoever gives their allegiance to Him, and I believe I am correct to say the God of creation protects His people from the hurt the unbelievers will experience.

> **Revelation 9:5** and it was <u>given</u> (means commanded) that <u>they</u> (the rebellious demon angels from Hell) should not kill <u>them</u> (the residents on Earth), but <u>they</u> should be tormented for five months.

Sometime before the five months in Revelation 9:15 has ended, the four angels are released from the Euphrates River, and the escalated killing begins, and they will slay the third part of men.

The next informative scripture doesn't exactly say five months, but it does seem to combine with the above scripture. Even though it doesn't give an exact number of months, the same way the Book of Revelation does, it implies the same message.

> **Mark 13:20** Jesus says, and except that the Lord had shortened <u>those days</u> (the tribulation days), no flesh should be saved. But for the *elects' sake*, <u>whom</u> <u>He</u> <u>hath</u> <u>chosen</u> (to save), He hath shortened the days.

Indeed, the wicked Lucifer and the other rebellious angels may get close to overcoming God's people, who have His seal on their forehead, just as they overcome the two witnesses. For this reason, the last three and one-half years will be shortened to five months.

Positively, the all-knowing Son of God tells us, it's shortened for the sake of His elect. But it'll not be shortened to five months because of an assumed rapture theory. This truth means Jesus is coming back thirty-seven months early, and it must be to save His people, who have His seal.

He's not coming back thirty-seven months early to save ungodly men guilty of having the mark of the beast on their forehead. But I am certain that God cares about His loyal, hot, and on-fire children and will protect them from demons.

The rapture theory seems to be a big expectation, with many Christians who believe in it without proof of its validity. But all Bible-savvy Christians should realize the rapture theory is an assumption, and there's no concrete proof of a prophesized rapture.

However, most Christians believe they'll float into the clouds and escape the great tribulation on this Earth. Sadly, it also appears most Christians do not believe the seal of God on their forehead will protect them from the rebellious demons from Hell.

Therefore, without sincere faith in God and the seal of God, a person will want to believe in the rapture theory, and as a majority, most Christians believe in the rapture philosophy. I am sure the rapture philosophy is a weak, unproven philosophy the understudied believe in wholeheartedly.

However, regardless of the rapture philosophy's weakness, most Christians believe they'll float into the clouds before the great tribulation time begins. I warn you: do not put all your eggs into this basket philosophy, but live godly and receive the seal of God and depend on His protection.

However, if the tribulation time does begin, the rapture believers discover that they haven't floated into the clouds to be with Jesus. Then they'll have to ask themselves a serious question since they are still here and haven't turned lightweight and flown away like a leaf in the wind.

The important question needs an answer. What are God's *elect* and chosen ones still doing here, and why did they believe in a rapture theory not written into the scriptures? When no one floats into the air, it will be a shot-down hindsight question, obviously answered by point-blank reality.

However, for the benefit of the believers in Christ, He has shortened the last half of the tribulation time to five months. The shortness is designed for the elect's sake, whom He'll spare from witnessing the terribleness of extreme evil.

Indeed, these informative words are taken from the Book of Revelation, Mark, and the prophecy, spoken from the mouth of Yeshua. It means these prophesized words aren't speculation spoken by just anyone.

It's for certain, Jesus says, no flesh shall be saved unless the last three and one-half years of the tribulation days are shortened to five months mainly because Lucifer and the rebellious supernatural angels could easily kill every inferior creation living on this Earth in forty-two months.

Especially if the last three and one-half years of the tribulation time aren't shortened to five months, and the analogy we have to assume from the words of Jesus is a message of death and destruction. The God of creation will forcefully shorten the last thirty-seven months, and the seven years of tribulation will not be for seven years.

Indeed, Lucifer and the rebellious angels intend to kill all the living flesh on this Earth before the Son of God returns, except for the female, whom they may let live for a little while because of her significant ability to reproduce children.

This truth means the rebellious angels can use her to start their mixed bloodline again and fill the Earth with their children again for the second time. The same way they did during the first Earth age, before the great flood, when they killed the flesh and blood males.

Conclusively, I advise you to have trust and faith in the seal of God for divine protection, and when Satan is close to overcoming the seal of God, Christ will return at the right moment. I have the faith to believe He'll save His believers, sealed with His seal, and I hope you share the same faith.

However, I want you to know it's silly to believe Christians will float into the clouds to meet Yeshua and then believe He'll turn around and take them to Heaven and not come back again until the end of the tribulation time.

I assure you He'll be sticking around when He comes from Heaven and will be one of the reapers, and no one will be raptured out ahead of time. But the rebellious angels and the evil Lucifer will become inferior when He returns.

Before this story ends, I want to reveal an important scripture to the rapture believers.

> **Matthew 13:30** Let both grow together until the harvest: and in the time of the harvest I will say to the reapers, gather ye together *first* the tares, and bind them in bundles to burn them: but gather the wheat into my barn.

The tares are the children of Satan, the mark of the beast children, and they will be reaped *first*. This truth means the wheat, the children of God, will not float into the clouds, but they'll stay here and be residents of the thousand-year millennium.

Indeed, we better hope we are exempt from being reaped first by the sickle in the hands of the reaper angels who bundle the tares first and cast them into the fire. But let's be the wheat the reaper angels save and gather into His barn.

CHAPTER EIGHTEEN

INDEED, SAVED

I want you to realize that being saved from the judgment fire and converted into a new person should be everyone's priority in this life. But you should also know attending a church building or a meeting place isn't one of the necessities to getting and staying saved.

Furthermore, we can spend days searching through the scriptures meticulously, and there's no place within our informative Bible where my great God tells us we must attend a specific type of building before we can be saved and stay saved.

For this reason, I want you to know that if the Holy Ghost lives within our hearts, our heart is God's living church; I guarantee no church or temple building can replace the living church of God. As incredible as it sounds, you must realize the living church of God is made from flesh, and it's our flesh.

This revealing story, *Indeed, Saved*, isn't popular with most preachers and priests, and it's because most churches insist we gather at a building on Sun-day morning. Truthfully, I knowingly conclude men's tradition is to gather at a building on Sunday morning.

However, just maybe, too much priority is put on a church building and the Sunday morning Sabbath Day when the real priority should be put on the required word of God and how we conform to His rules and the authentic Sabbath Day He declared from the beginning.

I guarantee the meaningful word of God isn't contained in a manmade building, nor is the Holy Ghost contained inside a building. But the word of God and the ever-available Holy Ghost can be found anywhere in this world if we seek to find them.

Therefore, a failure to find them lies upon the shoulders of each individual, who is unaware of their presence and understanding. Indeed, seeking and finding responsibility will always be our obligation, and whenever we decide we want a new life, we must discuss it with God.

Before this story starts, I want to say that much knowledge about God can be found in the Sun-day churches. This truth means the good news is everywhere: devout men of God are gathered together, and it's good whenever men assemble themselves and teach each other the beautiful gospel of God.

Furthermore, I believe much good is accomplished in many Sun-day churches, even if they have flaws in some doctrines. As much as we wish all Christian churches preached perfect authenticity, sadly, they do not, so we must study the gospel ourselves.

However, I want you to know that Sun-day churches and stationary gathering places are one option among other great choices, especially since we do not have to attend a church building to have a Savior and be saved and stay saved.

Sometimes, church groups think they provide the only way to find and understand God, and this misconception isn't true at all. I am certain we'll find Christians who never walk through a church door, much more Bible-savvy than members inside a church building.

For example, this example can portray the imagination of a great prophet of God who accomplished great works for the glory of God. Elijah thought he was the only prophet left alive in Israel, determined to fight against the wicked Ahab, Jezebel, and the false god Baal.

Therefore, God said unto Elijah, I have seven thousand other servants who haven't bowed down to Baal. I am willing to believe that the living church of God parallels the seven thousand existing outside the walls of a stationary building, and it's the largest church of God.

In the churches and temples, appearances seem to matter much to most professing Sun-day Christians. But when we belong to God's redefined living church, our appearance only matters to God, and being a loyal believer in God qualifies us as a member of the living church of God.

Mainly because He sees the real you and me, not veiled by fake smiles, deceiving words, and expensive clothing. When we are alone at home worshipping our wonderful God, the authentic you and I are real, and our character isn't fake.

I guarantee that my Great Supernatural Creator God cannot be deceived, and false appearances do not work in the living church of God. But because its members are loyal and love God, they gladly follow the teaching of the living Holy Ghost, who guides their thoughts.

Positively, I want you to know that my wonderful Creator God is the preacher behind the pulpit, teaching within the living church of God, and counterfeit appearances or insincere words cannot deceive my Great God. I assure you, my sincere God does not deceive anyone, and nothing about Him is fake.

Therefore, as shocking as it sounds to many Christians, Going to a Sun-day church made from wood, stone, and metal is unimportant. But it's vitally important and an absolute requirement for every professing Christian to belong to the living church of God.

People belonging to the living church of God will eat mana from Heaven and drink pure water flowing from His throne. They'll receive the keys to His peaceful kingdom, walk and talk, and live among the saved in Heaven.

However, we cannot say that everyone from the Sun-day churches and temples is saved and will receive a home in His special kingdom. But we can say that everyone belonging to God's living church is saved from the condemnation of damnation.

This truth means everyone belonging to the living church of God will be rewarded with the grand prize of immortality. The reward of immortality has a connection with my Great Creator God and not with a manmade building where men teach the traditions of men.

Therefore, the only way to be certain we are saved, an absolute child of God, and will receive the gift of eternal life. It's to belong to the living church of God, a special, intangible, and real church where the Holy Ghost is our one-on-one teacher with every member.

I assure you the wonderful Holy Ghost is the Great Preacher on this Earth, and He dwells within every hot and on-fire believer in Christ if they have a clean temple suitable for the righteous and special Holy Ghost to dwell within. But for Him to dwell within a believer in Christ, please realize it's important for the habitation place of the Holy Ghost to be clean.

There's no doubt in my mind when the great preacher from the book of Ecclesiastes gave us the conclusion to the whole matter. Then, the wonderful Holy Ghost of God gave him the conclusion to the whole matter.

Furthermore, it's easy for me to conclude when the great preacher man in the Old Testament illustrated his wisdom, summed up the whole word of God, and said it's the whole duty of man to reverence God and keep His Commandments.

Then, I believe, the wonderful Holy Ghost of God was responsible for giving the great preacher man his brilliant words of wisdom to preach and teach to all men and women on this Earth. As for myself, I know the wonderful Holy Ghost shares wisdom with you and me to some unknown degree, as He did with the great preacher.

Beyond the shadow of a doubt, the ultimate message, the conclusion to the whole matter, has an urgent mission in life to accomplish. It's the greatest and the most important message in our Bible and should be preached to all men, women, and children everywhere.

Mainly because it's the wonderful message of salvation and the formula for immortality, and it reveals all our requirements. Please realize everything God gives us hinges on the conclusion to the whole matter, and all our important decisions in this life should hinge on the word of God, too.

I assure you, every message and every story the God of Heaven and Earth, Yeshua, and the prophets wrote between Genesis and Revelation point to the wonderful message, the conclusion to the whole matter. Everything Yehovah, the Son of God, and the prophets taught all point to the conclusion of the whole matter.

However, I want you to know if we fall short of living by God's whole word and make mistakes, we desire to correct ourselves and get right with the God of Heaven and Earth. Then, God's beautiful grace allows us to repent, change, and be forgiven.

Positively, God's wonderful and caring Son voluntarily suffered death on the cross and gave His life, so we'll have the privilege to amend mistakes. He knows we'll make mistakes, and He also knows if we are remorseful for making them or not remorseful.

However, Conversion, repentance, and change mean we desire to live our lives according to the conclusion to the whole matter. Truly, if we live according to the conclusion to the whole matter, we fulfill our obligation to our Savior God and are saved.

Furthermore, it's regardless of the church or the home we worship within because abiding by the conclusion to the whole matter is the main thing. I want you to know living by the conclusion to the whole matter has a parallel, and living by the ways of God is a parallel.

The conclusion to the whole matter is summed up in six words: reverence God and keep His commandments. This statement of truth means reverence to God, and keeping His commandments is the whole duty of men and angels.

Furthermore, whether we live on the Earth or dwell in the Heavens above, it's regardless. The wonderful conclusion to the whole matter will always be a requirement in both places. I want you to know that God's great commandments will be as important in the next life as they are now.

Conclusively, the wonderful prize of immortality is obtainable. We can depart this life as a winner of immortality, and it's because we try to keep the required commandments of God. I want you to realize keeping His commandments highlights His greatest expectation of us.

Beyond the shadow of a doubt, we illustrate reverence to Him because we are determined to live according to His righteous word. I want you to know the wonderful gift of grace doesn't mean we aren't bound to His required word because living by His word is the pinnacle of doing right.

This teaching story, *Indeed Saved*, reveals the weightier word of God is highly important information. Surely, knowing we are saved is comforting and much better than not knowing where we stand with our wonderful Creator God.

I assure you the bread of life is the exact word of God, and saved people love the word of God the same way bees love honey. Since I am in love with the word of God, then you could call me a honey lover. But it's for certain the righteous word of God is sweeter than honey.

CHAPTER NINETEEN

THE REASON FOR ALL SIN

Have you ever asked yourself, what is the reason for sin, and does it boil down to one specific thing? What if you, I, and the whole world knew the exact reason for sin? Would knowing this truth make a difference to everyone, and would sinners quit sinning?

Truly, ask yourself, would the whole world change if they knew the reason for sin and knew we could have a perfect world? I ask this question because stopping sin and all the ungodly things connected to sin would be the greatest achievement known to mankind.

Stopping sin would be the greatest economic boast in this world, and stopping sin would simplify this distressful and complicated world. Stopping sin would eliminate fraud, dishonesty, and covenanting, and thanks to the beautiful gospel of God, stopping sin would end all the bad things people do.

This God-inspired story concerning the moral direction of this world is called *The Reason For All Sin*. It illuminates the one specific thing entwined with all acts of sin, and even if everyone in the world will not change for the better, will you quit sinning and change?

In this truer than a straight arrow, we need to understand the story; it reveals rebellion against the word of God as the number one cause of every problem in this world. Truly, rebellion against God's righteous word was the problem between the corrupt angels and God and is the problem between the rebellious man and God.

I want you to know the beautiful and righteous Ten Commandments of God, consisting of approximately two hundred and ninety-five words, are the pinnacle of perfection. If we kept them all and our world revolved around them, we would have a great world to live in forever.

God makes it clear through His first excellent commandment, telling us He's the only God worth acknowledging and worshipping. Indeed, within His first commandment, He uses the word god to emphasize that this world will have many self-proclaimed gods.

I believe our Most High God knows everyone in our world knows Him, or at least has heard about Him. But my Great God also knows that not everyone will accept Him as their personal God, regardless of illogical reasons.

Even though most rebellious men know He's the only Supreme Creator God, and they know He holds the keys to immortality. Still, they refuse to put their trust in Him and reject Him for the ways of the rebellious fallen angels, who rejected Him in Heaven.

Indeed, it's because rebellious men do not want to live by the rules of God, and not any more than the rebellious angels did. It could be possible their rebellious nature is inherited from a previous Earth age or Heavenly age, and they cannot overcome their inherited nature.

The fact is true: the wicked Lucifer, alias Satan, the Devil, the Serpent of Old, is the wicked prince of this world. Deceptively, through the names of so many gods, rebellion is multiplied throughout all four corners of this Earth, but under alias names.

Therefore, all the lesser gods on this Earth, with their many different names, are aliases, Lucifer in disguise, regardless of what name or nation these gods use as their base nation. It's quite obvious different gods have many servants who worship them, and these worshippers are lost souls submissive to the power of Satan.

This truth means Lucifer's wicked spirit can influence and manifest himself in his puppet servants anywhere the weak man stands. Regardless of the name his servants are called or the nation they live within, he influenced and entered Judas Iscariot similarly.

Apparently, through the use of various names, deception is accomplished, and the art of deception is his greatest skill. The art of deception illustrates Lucifer's way of tricking many people and wayward nations into worshipping him as a divine god, and sadly, the heathens rage under the influence of Satan.

Even though the heathen's worship is performed through an alias named god or even a female goddess, it's still an alias god who follows and observes his evil and wicked ways of rebellion. Sadly, we can be certain that God's perfect word isn't their doctrine, and following Him isn't their desire.

Indeed, this is one reason why worshiping only Him is emphasized in God's first commandment. I assure you, our Great Creator God is warning us, and our Bible says not to have any other gods before our God, called Yehovah, Israel's great and righteous God.

Furthermore, we can search through every commandment of God and find evidence warning us about the consequences of being rebellious to His word. Indeed, concrete evidence of rebellion always attaches to breaking His perfect Ten Commandments.

Commandment keeping is vital; the gift of eternal life hinges on the observance of God's great Ten Commandments. This fact alone highlights the powerful Ten Commandments more valuable than all other words, and we should write them on the doorposts of our houses.

I assure you, foolishness and nonsense, such as recognizing other gods and making statues and pictures of them. Including the making of images of creations in the Heavens above or the Earth beneath, could cause the loss of salvation through our Supreme God.

Mainly because the worship, or even the recognition of counterfeit gods and goddesses, are the works of darkness, and the works of darkness branch back to the evil Lucifer and to the first Earth age before the great flood.

I assure you the works of darkness, committed throughout every generation, are all accomplished through the spirit of rebellion. I firmly believe all our bad characteristics are expressed through the spirit of rebellion, and committing acts of rebellion means we are doing something contrary to the gospel of God.

I am certain that the terrible spirit of rebellion is entwined with the wicked spirit of Lucifer, and our Bible indicates the evil Lucifer is the spirit of darkness. Undoubtedly, rebellion against righteousness began with him and will not end until he's destroyed.

Therefore, when men bow down, they worship and serve other gods and make pagan altars to illustrate their recognition of a false god. It's a bold and matter-of-fact statement, and they're saying they do not believe in Yehovah and do not want Him as their Most High God.

Truly, servitude to other gods and goddesses and rejection of our Great Creator God's ways could be seen as pure ignorance. But maybe a rejection of God goes beyond the spectrum of ignorance, and it's pure hate or a combination of both; you decide.

It's hard for me to imagine anyone hating God, but not all men feel the same about God as I do. However, it's obvious through eyesight some men appear to hate God, even though hating God is as illogical as swimming in deep water with a gang of sharks.

Indeed, because various gods are being worshipped worldwide, it's easy to conclude spiritual blindness is incurable sometimes. However, for some illogical reason, many men and women both turn away from our wonderful Creator God and foolishly choose to recognize, embrace, and serve the ways of self-proclaimed lesser gods.

Therefore, the fact remains accurate whether it's spoken hate, unspoken hate, or expressed through false god worship. This truth means rebellion against our Great Creator God indicates hate, and I want you to know the wicked Lucifer is the root cause of hate.

It's extremely disrespectful to God when men bow their knees before any image, and worshipping an image, a picture of an alias god, or a strange rock that fell from the Heavens above is the most sinful thing anyone can do. All false god worshippers need to know nations worldwide that bow before manufactured gods are restricted from entering the kingdom of God.

Especially if they know the wonderful God of Israel is the Supreme Almighty Creator God of Heaven and Earth and know about His Bible stories from the past, who know His history and realize He does supernatural miracles for the people He loves.

The descendants of Ishmael and Esau are the guiltiest rebellious people among all the people on this Earth, mainly because they know the difference between God and gods. Yet, the rebellious part of them defies God, and they still worship unproven gods, such as Dagon and Allah.

Even though they know the history concerning some of the miracles of our Most High God of Israel, this means rebellion against Yehovah is the only logical conclusion that explains their worship of counterfeit gods.

Indeed, hate is expressed by anyone who knows the truth and opposes the truth and the source of the truth. It's an undebatable fact; the reason for all sin amounts to rebellion against the required word of God.

The jealous descendants of Ishmael and Esau hate our Supreme God, mostly because of their lesser inheritance from Abraham and Isaac. Sadly, they are jealous, like Cain, who hated his brother Abel.

Without a doubt, hate and rebellion against God's perfect word are the two main things causing sin. I want you to know that if our Great God abhors anything, He abhors rebellion, hate, and worship of other gods.

I assure you when He illustrates wrath, it's usually provoked by rebellion and hate. Surely, our Great God's reaction to sin illuminates the importance of keeping the excellent Ten Commandments.

The perfect and righteous Ten Commandments of God have great power, and I am certain they divert the wrath of God. Truly, I want you to realize that every one of them is a deterrent, advising us not to sin against His beautiful commandments.

The perfect Ten Commandments are our moral barometer, and they indicate how well, or how terrible, we are doing with God. The required Ten Commandments are our main law for our benefit and will not change from generation to generation.

Therefore, I want you to know for certain and not be ignorant of this important knowledge. The excellent and dividing Ten Commandments of God will present us as a lawful or lawless person before the Lord someday.

I assure you, no manmade law of the land supersedes the law of the Ten Commandments of God in His courtroom. This truth means it's regardless of whether or not we decide to live by them or separate ourselves from them.

Because of their perfection, they'll still judge us in the coming time, and our souls will hang in the balance between eternal life and damnation.

Truly, I want you to know the Ten Commandments parallel the Ten God-inspired Judges we face daily, which do not bend from the original.

Furthermore, many professing Christians wrongly believe the commandments of God have been done away with and aren't valid anymore. Sadly, they believe this way because there's not enough enthusiasm for the word of God, false preaching, and false teaching within the churches of God.

Indeed, many Christians would like to do away with the Ten Commandments of God as much as the unbelievers do because it would relieve them of their compromises. Disregarding them allows them room to do ungodly things and not be held accountable for doing them.

Mainly because no commandments to live by have advantages to lukewarm Christians, and no commandments mean no more sin, no more lawlessness, and no more accountability. However, it's absurd to think we can have a lawless world without moral guidelines to keep us in check.

Beyond the shadow of a doubt, many Christians believe wrongly concerning the beautiful and righteous Ten Commandments being nailed to the cross, and I firmly believe it's mostly because of Bible ignorance due to a lack of understudy. I warn you: a man or woman unwilling to increase their knowledge of God is foolish and will perish for lack of Bible knowledge.

Therefore, many Christians will say no one's perfect, or they'll say the grace of God saves us, and their assumption is expressed and misguided because they are unlearned about God's righteous and truthful ways.

Mainly because they've been taught false doctrines from within many churches and the temples of God, and for this reason, we should be Bible savvy and wise or wiser than the preacher man. We are foolish to put all our trust in another man's teaching or believe the gift of grace is all we need.

Indeed, I know for certain false teaching leads Christians astray from the right way. However, I do not know for certain whether or not false teaching within the church will be excusable before the eyes of God and mercy will prevail. Although I know our Bible tells us that a lack of Bible knowledge will be why some men and women perish.

Furthermore, it's easy to conclude false teaching seems to have a domino effect; in the same way, fire spreads in a strong wind. It's certain false teaching will do incalculable harm to our relationship with God, so we should study the Bible for ourselves.

Positively, I also know free men who hunger for the beautiful word of God and desire to understand the required word of God are the believers who trust in Him. Also, hungry God lovers usually make ample time to read the Bible for themselves if they can read.

This truth means men and women who can read do not have to depend entirely on the interpretation of preachers and teachers for their increased knowledge. Truly, the more we study the commanded word of God, the more secure our salvation.

Furthermore, I assure you, our excellent Holy Ghost of God is a much better teacher than any flesh and blood preacher man, and I want you to realize the Holy Ghost warns our conscience when the thoughts of our hearts start considering the desire to sin. Always remember keeping the dwelling place of the Holy Ghost clean means our knowledge and power of discernment will increase by many folds.

Conclusively, all sin happens when we stray away from the perfect Ten Commandments of God. This informative story, *The Reason For All Sin,* points to rebellion against the great Ten Commandments of God.

This serious story we all need to understand, *The Reason For All Sin*, is an awareness story, and it's saying the caring Ten Commandments of God can prevent all sin. I am certain preventing sin will secure us a dwelling place in the kingdom of God.

However, I want you to know that breaking the great Ten Commandments puts our gift of salvation in danger. All types of sin entwine with breaking the required Ten Commandments of God, and an alarm should sound inside our head when we compromise His word.

I assure you, the perfect bread of life isn't made from flour or cornmeal, but the bread of life will always be God's excellent and perfect word. Because it's necessary, I hope you fall in love with the word of God, and you'll become a hot and on-fire Christian, not lukewarm or passive.

CHAPTER TWENTY

GAMBLING ENTWINED WITH MERCY

This informative story, *Gambling Entwined With Mercy*, explores the unknown boundaries of my great God, mainly because we, flesh and blood men and women, do not know the boundary line where mercy ends and wrath begins. For this reason, let's not be gamblers.

Indeed, this serious story, *Gambling Entwined With Mercy*, advises everyone to proceed cautiously through this life. Let's not be passive and waste time taking chances between salvation and damnation by being foolish, unlearned, and haphazardly.

This extremely serious story is meant to portray a gamble when men stray from the Ten Commandments of God. This truth means we do not know the full extent of God's mercy, nor are we wise enough to know the boundary line of no return.

Therefore, I ask you, will the many unlearned and rebellious men guilty of rebelling against the commandments of God be granted mercy due to Bible ignorance? Furthermore, I ask you, will we be able to plead ignorance before the Judgment Throne of God and be granted mercy?

I suppose there are many reasons for scripture ignorance and lack of enthusiasm for Bible study concerning the excellent word of God. But realize God reads the heart of every person, and He's aware of valid and invalid excuses for lack of Bible knowledge.

Therefore, I want you to know He can and will judge between justifiable and unjustifiable Bible ignorance. However, mercy will be easier to obtain through justifiable Bible ignorance. But I warn you, pleading Bible ignorance is a high-stakes gamble.

However, it's not my place to judge why men do not follow or believe in keeping the righteous commandments of God. Although, I will say it's not wise to oppose or neglect the things able to make a difference between salvation and damnation.

Especially since we aren't aware and do not know the boundary line between mercy, forgiveness, and un-forgiveness, why should we gamble on our salvation and a home in the kingdom of God when we know for certain salvation is too important to gamble with at all?

Especially since all we have to do to preserve our gift of salvation is to follow His beautiful Ten Commandments and reverence Him, and we can imagine the boundary line of mercy. Still, any assumption we conclude other than commandment keeping will be similar to thinking ice will not melt in the sunshine.

Therefore, our definition of mercy should be the same definition God attaches to His definition of mercy, and if it's not, mercy might be as hard to obtain as a cold glass of water in a hot desert. I want to warn you that abusing the gift of mercy would be a mistake, and some are irreversible.

The next easy-to-understand scripture reveals the absolute word of God, and it eliminates assumptions and imaginations concerning the definition of mercy. So, we'll know without guessing the next extremely serious scripture reveals who is granted mercy from the God of Heaven and Earth.

However, before I tell you the answer, I know no one is perfect on this Earth, and we all fall short of God's expectations. I believe we may be a perfectionist in the next life, but for now, we aren't perfectionists and will make mistakes.

Therefore, I hope and pray that you and I will be one of His special people who are granted the gift of mercy because you and I love God and try to be faithful with all our hearts to keep His excellent commandments.

I am certain the next informative scripture erases the guesswork of putting a definition to the mercy of God. I want you to realize that the words in the next scripture are His words of iron, and because of their importance to our souls, I want you to know that the next scripture is as important as drinking water and should be remembered daily.

> **Exodus 20:6** (The word of God says), and *showing mercy* unto thousands of them that love <u>Me</u> (Yehovah), and keep My commandments.

Without a doubt, we cannot be perfect Christians, but we can refuse to be rebellious to the required word of God. Thanks to the blood sacrifice of Yeshua, by the grace of God, we can repent, change, and re-adjust when we discover we are living in opposition to the beautiful word of God.

The God of Heaven and Earth will forgive us and show us mercy if we humbly recognize and admit our mistakes and return to the right path. Indeed, my loving God knows we battle with His number one enemy, Lucifer, alias Satan, the deceiving Serpent of Old.

Therefore, God patiently waits for us to overcome sin and rebellion, and how long He'll wait, I do not know. But I know most of my righteous God's promises to Christians have requirements, and we would be foolish to think otherwise or to believe Commandment keeping isn't necessary to claim promises.

His promises are obtained and can be claimed by us simply by loving Him and keeping His Ten Commandments. The above scripture proves the gift of mercy can be added to the promises of God because we love Him and keep His guiding commandments.

However, I do not find any exceptions to the promise of God, allowing for rebellion, hate, and servitude to other gods. But most likely, Bible illiteracy is due to understudy, lack of interest, or too many diversion options, and Satan creates diversions in the hope of twisting our footsteps and tricking us into compromising the beautiful gospel of God.

Indeed, we will compromise His word if the desire in our hearts isn't strong enough to overcome the evil spirits of the air, which cause spiritual blindness. Undoubtedly, spiritual blindness is caused by unbelief since unbelief is the major symptom pointing to spiritual blindness, and no exceptions mean spiritual blindness isn't acceptable.

Therefore, unbelief, or not enough belief in Him, could be reason enough to revoke the gracious gift of mercy, especially since the scriptures say mercy is only shown to those who love my supreme God and keep His perfect commandments.

From the beginning of the God-inspired Bible until the last chapter of the Bible, including every generation living on this Earth, keeping the Ten Commandments is undoubtedly an unchallengeable analogy, revealing the greatest message in our Bible.

However, I want you to realize the second greatest message in our Bible coincides with the first greatest message God wants His people to know. Truly, rebellion to our Bible's first and second greatest message reveals the reason for all sin.

Reverence illustrated to God is the first greatest message in our Bible, and keeping His commandments is the second greatest message He wants us to know. This truth means mercy from above is a gift to everyone determined to reverence God and keep His beautiful commandments.

In the above sentence, I purposely use the expression, beautiful commandments because of their importance and because my Great Creator God's commandments can create a wonderful world. The Ten Commandments are the pinnacle of beauty since nothing ever written compares to them.

Indeed, a wonderful world where everyone's character is perfected by His perfect Ten Commandments illuminates the dream God dreams. A wonderful world is a special place where weapons, locks, guard dogs, and high fences aren't necessary for the residents of His kingdom.

I assure you that the above two messages from God, the apostles, and the Son of God are firm and unchangeable. And all Christians will always be required to love God as their Father, who desires to create a perfect society.

Furthermore, keeping the Ten Commandments proves overwhelming love for God and the desire to improve our character. The conclusion to the whole matter concerning the beautiful gift of salvation is to love God and keep His required commandments.

Fear and reverence for our creator God are positively illustrated and proven sincere through obedience to His required word. This truth means, beyond the shadow of a doubt, that disobedience has the same definition as being rebellious to our covenant with God.

I assure you, all acts of rebellion prove a parallel point that's unchangeable. The parallel point means commandment breakers demonstrate a lack of love, a lack of respect, a lack of fear, and a lack of reverence for our wonderful Most High Creator God.

Furthermore, it appears that certain rebellious men and women, including the rebellious angels, have a love for God problem. They lack the kind of obedient character the Ten Commandments are trying to create so that they can be acceptable to the society of God.

Therefore, if we want to live forever and be able to come and go through the Gates of Pearl as we please, then we better reverence God and keep His commandments. The Bible assures us commandment keeping is what God expects from you and me.

Furthermore, please be warned that rebellion against the required word of God gains us nothing in the next life. This truth means the gift of salvation isn't automatic, and He will not allow rebellious men and women entrance into His kingdom.

Please remember these extremely serious next words every night and every day and never forget them. The reason for all sin and the habitation place called Hell is rebellion against God's perfect, righteous, and wonderful word.

Furthermore, the beautiful gift of mercy is given to whosoever is loyal, loves God, and keeps His perfect Ten Commandments. Truly, I want you to know it's a myth to believe our Great and Righteous God will not withhold His mercy and not send anyone to Hell.

Indeed, He certainly will withhold His mercy, and the wicked Lucifer and the rebellious angels are examples of rebellious creations already living in Hell. Another excellent example of a person being sent to hell is the rich man in the story of Lazarus.

Furthermore, the residents of Sodom and Gomorrah, whom God destroyed with fire and brimstone, are undoubtedly in Hell with Lucifer. Assuredly, the wide road going through the wide gate is wide because of an overwhelming amount of traffic going to Hell.

Indeed, our God-inspired Bible reveals that Hell has enlarged itself to accommodate an unnumbered number of people not invited to live in the kingdom of God. Truly, it's correct to say everyone living in the terrible place called Hell didn't obtain mercy from the God of creation.

CHAPTER TWENTY-ONE

BREAD FROM THE TABLE OF LUCIFER

This need to consider the story, *Bread From Lucifer's Table*, reveals enlightenment and is a need-to-know story. It highlights two specific things we'll always find on the table of Lucifer, and after you read this story, you'll be forced to realize many people are eating from the table of Lucifer.

This need-to-understand message is a literal and metaphoric story, including food on the table and sinful characteristics. But this absolutely serious story begins with the literal, and I am talking about food on the table, and to be more specific, the literal is the food we consume.

Therefore, if we eat unclean foods, we aren't supposed to eat them because God told us not to eat them. Then it's the same thing as us eating the bread from Lucifer's table, and we are eating from his table because we aren't obeying the written word of God.

For the above reason, eating the bread from Lucifer's table also means we are doing something Lucifer would want us to do rather than doing what God wants us to do. I want you to know whenever we compromise the word of God, we eat the bread from Lucifer's table.

Therefore, when I use the word bread, I use it as a literal word for meat, unclean to eat, and a symbolic word for anything ungodly. As for the literal unclean, I'll try and put myself in another person's shoes and illustrate the results of eating the unclean swine's flesh.

Indeed, I'll use myself as an example in these next few verses and illustrate disobedience to God's excellent word. The kind of disobedience used to cause uncleanness to the soul and the heart of every living temple of God.

For example, consider that I place myself in the unclean man's shoes because I wouldn't listen to my Superior God. Because I oppose His superior wisdom, I've decided the literal unclean isn't important to God, and because the smell and taste are good, I will overlook His advice.

Therefore, opposing His wisdom means I've decided to eat the forbidden unclean abominations the God of creation instructed me not to eat. Furthermore, I am unclean because of my foolishness at the dinner table, set before me with unclean foods.

This truth means my foolishness at the dinner table makes me an unclean abomination before the eyes of my clean and holy God. My rejection to put a difference between the clean and the unclean and my failure to obey the perfect word of God means I am a compromiser of the word of God, and my body will suffer because I eat the unclean.

It also means I've willingly sinned against His word and have fallen short of His expectations to be a clean person for His glorious Holy Ghost to live within. All because I ate the unclean swine, and after eating it, I was made unfit and too detestable for the Holy Ghost to live within me.

Therefore, I am made unclean by the unholy and disgusting unclean beast animal, possessed through and through by uncleanness. This truth means the foods you and I eat matter to the God of Heaven and Earth much more than we might think it matters.

Without a doubt, a lack of Bible knowledge or concern about unclean foods leaves men and women with the excuse to say; I didn't know any better. But sadly, not knowing any better is our fault and partially the fault of our preachers and parents.

Indeed, our preachers and parents didn't teach us the clean ways of our Great God and the gospel truth concerning unclean foods in our youth. Truly, these things concerning the unclean are vitally important if we want to keep our living temple clean.

However, I am certain our wonderful Creator God's teaching word only matters to a devout professing Christian who desires to obey and please the God of creation and keep the Holy Ghost a clean dwelling place. Sadly, we fail the Holy Ghost when His temple is unclean because of our eating habits.

This truth means the unbelievers and the servants of Satan do not have to live godly as Christians must obey His laws. The unbelievers can eat all the unclean swine they want to eat and not be bothered concerning staying clean for the presence of the Holy Ghost.

It is because staying clean, holy, and pleasing to the God of creation doesn't matter to the unbelievers; if it did, they would be believers in Christ. But sadly to say, it's their delight to eat bread and consume the swine flesh from the table of Lucifer.

I assure you the table of Lucifer, the temple of Lucifer, and the unclean world of Lucifer is a living empire full of uncleanness and abominations. His empire is identified as demonic, satanic, detestable, and disgusting, and a fly is caught in the trap when it eats the unclean.

Truly, the unclean swine illustrates a fitting definition of all the negative things symbolic of Lucifer in every aspect of uncleanness. I believe the swine's flesh is the meat upon his table, and the swine is the choice of meat for his children of darkness.

Therefore, whenever anyone eats the bread from the table of Lucifer, it's like being a part of his body and a member of the living unclean. I assure you, everything considered an abomination to the Lord is a part of the unclean flock, and the unclean flock eats from the table of Lucifer.

Beyond the shadow of a doubt, the unclean flock together like birds of a feather, playing together in the pool of sin. Furthermore, please keep in mind and understand the feelings of our wisest of the wise Lord as I put a definition to the word abomination.

Indeed, our wonderful Christian God hates abominations and desires us to keep a clean dwelling place for the Holy Ghost, and when our hearts are clean, His perfect Spirit can talk to and teach from within us. However, maybe His Spirit cannot teach from within an unclean temple, and why would the Spirit of God live in an unclean temple?

Furthermore, He defines abominations as disgusting, detestable, unclean, polluting, and ungodly, and the definition of unclean swine is detestable and disgusting by nature. For one disgusting reason: the unclean swine will eat their feces as long as they live.

Therefore, the unclean swine cannot be considered a clean animal in this second Earth age, and it's because, our Great God says, it's not a clean animal. Truly, all unclean animal abominations in this world are unclean literal abominations to eat.

Conclusively, before this story ends, I ask you to look closely at a pig pen and watch the swine relieve himself in it. Then watch the swine root the piss up and eat it all day, then convince me the filthy swine is a clean and fit animal to eat.

The metaphoric part of this story includes sinful characteristics, and I am telling you that compromises to the word of God are unclean to the soul. I ask you, how could we consider acts of sin any different than uncleanness?

CHAPTER TWENTY-TWO

ABOMINATIONS ENTWINED WITH THE CORRUPT TREE

This exposure story concerns an important subject everyone should understand: *Abominations Entwined With The Corrupt Tree*. It has a declaration to declare and threads backward throughout the corridor of time to the beginning of mankind and the roots of evil.

The serious declaration, I gladly declare, ties all uncleanness and abominations to the tree of knowledge of good and evil, at least in a symbolic way. This declaration means the literal unclean is characterized similarly to the symbolic unclean, and similarities are undeniable, concerning parallels.

Indeed, both types of uncleanness are an abomination, even though they are different types of abominations. I declare that most literal abominations have a symbolic definition, and the symbolic definition is symbolic of the character and the image of Lucifer.

The literal abominations concerning all sorts of ungodliness also characterize the image of the wicked, rebellious angels fallen from Heaven and the corrupt tares whom Lucifer and the rebellious angels planted on this Earth to choke out and destroy the wheat.

I assure you, anything planted on this Earth to choke out or hinder the wheat is an evil abomination and has an ungodly and unclean image. Mainly because all types of abominations, including symbolic unclean abominations, mirror the character of Lucifer.

The mirror reflection of abominations also includes his demonic army of rebellious and wicked angels. All ungodly men and women, guilty of doing abominable works, are bitter fruit, and they parallel with the works of Lucifer and the misery of his nature.

Truly, I am certain the unrepented and unchanged tares planted here on this Earth are an ungodly abomination, and it's natural through heritage. Sadly, being clean and godly isn't important to the wicked tares, and since the beginning of creation, the tares have been an enemy of the wheat.

The literal swine is an unclean abomination to the food chain, and it's as hurtful as the tares are to the wheat. The swine's greatest useful purpose probably benefits the wicked dark prince of this world the most since it restricts the helping hand of the Holy Ghost.

Positively, the literal unclean swine doesn't benefit the children of God, but it hinders them if they eat it. Truly, if the children of God eat the swine's flesh, they are making their hearts unclean, and their heart is supposedly the dwelling place of the Holy Ghost.

I assure you, and you need to realize, regardless of whether it's the literal unclean or the sinful kind of unclean. One abomination is nearly as bad as the other since both types are disgusting. However, I willingly believe committing sinful acts would be less glamorous for us to do if we had a clean heart.

Indeed, all abominations can turn the clean into the unclean and create distance between our wonderful God and us. This statement says that the Father, the Son, and the Holy Ghost do not like the unclean. The unclean are fickle people, not trustworthy, and not loyal to God.

Most definitely, the root of all abominations leads to one source, and the source is the tree of knowledge of good and evil. All abominations grow and flourish and work in conjunction with Lucifer's unclean and wicked agenda. Surely, to quote a true paraphrase, cleanness is next to godliness.

Conclusively, I want you to realize the terrible Lucifer is this world's ungodly, wicked god, and Bible scriptures reveal he's the spirit prince of the air. Lucifer is the thief who kills, steals, and destroys, and he promotes ungodliness through uncleanness. Throughout every generation, uncleanness is the primary reason for literal uncleanness and sinful abominations.

I assure you he fertilizes abominations with immorality and carnal wickedness and promotes ungodliness, and because of him, sinful and lost souls worldwide do not try to live a moral, God-fearing, and righteous lifestyle.

However, because they live under the influence of demon angels, lost souls eat the bread and the meat from the table of Lucifer, and it seems they cannot break his grip on them. Sadly, they seem to enjoy the literal and the spiritual abominations, springing up from the tree of knowledge of good and evil.

I assure you: Lucifer is the corrupt tree, the Rebellious Serpent of Old, and the Unclean Abomination of Desolation. This short story, *Abominations Entwined With The Corrupt Tree*, connects everything evil to Lucifer and his army of demonic angels.

Indeed, I know that everything in this world has an origin and roots attached to a godly or ungodly source. As hard as it is for the understudied to believe, a beautiful angel from Heaven is the origin of all the negative things men and women do on this Earth.

I assure you that nothing evil, wicked, corrupt, or negative originated with the God of creation. But only the good things came from Him, and we should try hard to be Christ-like in all our endeavors since it doesn't make any sense to do otherwise.

This awareness story, *Abominations Entwined To The Corrupt Tree*, identifies all types of ungodliness as an unacceptable way to live. Truly, if my Great God were writing this story, He would say, stay clean and holy, as I Am, and do not eat the unclean swine.

CHAPTER TWENTY-THREE

INTERVIEWING MYSELF

I operated and owned a small construction business for most of my working life until I retired from a regular job, holding me to an everyday responsibility. After retiring from the workforce, I could pursue my lifelong dream and use words to express the love inside my heart for the gospel of God.

I am happy to tell you that my dream has always been to write beautiful, uplifting Bible stories in the simplest of language and put many definitions to the subject being talked about. Because I hunger for Bible knowledge, I want to write about every subject in the Bible and explain them in fullness.

I want you to know explaining Bible subjects in fullness is the greatest desire of my life. Explaining the word of God in detail is what I must do until the day I die because everyone needs to understand the meaning of the Bible's subjects concerning our lives.

After doing many interviews with other Christians, I've discovered that only a few people understand the exact word of God as they should. After doing many interviews, I finally realized that most people living in this Lucifer-controlled world are too Bible illiterate and will not study His word in-depth.

It also became obvious to me most people live from day to day lukewarm, passive, and indifferent. For some illogical reason, they do not seem to realize or care if they are being lukewarm toward the word of God, nor do they realize the consequences of profiling lukewarm or cold.

Truly, I've discovered there's not enough enthusiasm in this world for the wonderful word of God. This evaluation is a sad analogy but a true analogy, and it defies logic to be anything less than hot and on fire for the word of God since God expects us to be hot and on fire for His word.

Therefore, I conclude that most people prefer to do their own thing and do not seem to realize the importance of securing their eternal salvation. But for some illogical reason, they seem to believe the gift of salvation will automatically be given to them.

Furthermore, it seems that most people in this world have a blind problem in their thinking and are passive toward God's required word. Sadly, they haven't enough Bible knowledge to understand the dangerous repercussions of their lukewarm behavior.

Positively, and as illogical as it sounds, most people do not feel the need to explore the wonderful word of God intensely. But they'll read cookbooks, novels, and mushy love stories much more often than they do their Bible. Truly, learning how to cook many recipes is wonderful, but familiarizing yourself with the word of God is the most important.

Even when I talk to Christians about the Bible story books, I've written to enlighten and lift our Savior God. For an ununderstandable reason, most of them will ask me if my books are for children as if they already know all they need to know about my great God.

Truly, most people seem nonchalant about the requirements for eternal life, and only a few know about the Judgment Scales of God. However, not knowing about the Judgment Scales of God will take away some of the seriousness of our need to be Christ-like.

Apparently, for some illogical reason, being hot and on fire for the gospel of God doesn't seem necessary to most people. But it should, and our enthusiasm should equal hot and on fire as we journey through the rock slides and mud puddles of sin in this life.

I guarantee that all preachers and teachers should teach the importance of being hot and on fire for the word of God instead of teaching that the gift of grace is the key to eternal life. Surely, because of its importance to our souls, I believe being a hot and on fire Christian should entwine with conversion to Christianity.

Indeed, the gift of grace is wonderful, but it'll take a hot and on-fire Christian to hold onto the gift of grace. But most Christians I've interviewed believe grace is all they need, and for an ununderstandable reason, the gift of grace will cancel out everything sinful they do.

Furthermore, it appears that only a few Christians know the weightier matter of the important word of God, even though immortality is gained or lost, according to our lifestyle. But it still appears many Christians are passive and throw caution to the wind and do not realize that we better walk carefully and earn our salvation by doing right.

Furthermore, it appears factual, even if it's not completely true; most people seem to believe they can live a cold or lukewarm lifestyle, which will not hinder their gift of salvation through grace. Surely, this passive belief illustrates and reveals the definition of blind faith.

Therefore, I thought I would write a few Bible stories for fun, to increase learning and understanding, and to inspire love for His gospel. Since my first published book in July of 2011, I have nine published Bible storybooks and seventeen other unpublished books.

My nine published books amount to five hundred and twenty-nine individual Bible-related stories, consisting of one million and thirty-four thousand words. However, writing so many Bible stories and books wasn't something I planned to do, but I am glad to write stories involving God.

Positively, I never dreamed I would keep writing more and more stories, and a few stories would turn out to be so massive. But I kept writing more stories as if it were my calling in life. Now, I have another seven hundred hand-written Bible stories, none of which have been published.

It could be possible; I've written more Bible-related stories than any other individual, even since the beginning of life, and for God's glory, I hope to write many more stories. However, I believe my spirit will leave this Earth before they are published.

I am certain this unusual collection of Bible stories I've managed to write is unequaled by anyone in the literary world of Christianity. But I am also certain that most people living in this world who need to know about the God of salvation will never read my Bible-related stories or the God-inspired Bible.

This truth means most people will stand before our Great Creator God of Heaven and Earth someday, and they'll have a lack of knowledge about Him. Sadly, they'll not realize it matters until it's their turn to stand before Him at the Great Judgment Throne.

However, while I live and breathe, I fully intend to do my part and spread God's gospel to this starving world as much as possible, mainly because people need to understand their purpose in life, which is extremely serious. I will tell you, and everyone interested, that the whole duty of man is to live by His righteous Ten Commandments.

Furthermore, I want you to know that being a carefree and happy-go-lucky person will not enhance our purpose in this life. But being nonchalant will cause us to meet our Great God someday unprepared, which will be an unacceptable way to meet Him.

I assure you; this is a test ground Earth, and life in the flesh is short, and gaining eternal life depends on us becoming Disciples of Christ. But because of an indifferent attitude, most people worldwide are in trouble with God. Unfortunately, the carefree and happy-go-lucky people do not seem aware of their stance with Him.

Furthermore, throughout our beautiful Bible, our Great Creator God has presented us with His requirements for salvation, and we are fools if we do not take His eternal life requirements seriously. I assure you, His commandments aren't optional or bendable.

However, the question that needs to be answered is clear and seriously important. This truth means, can we trouble God by rejecting His requirements and then obtain the gift of salvation? I wouldn't gamble on it, but I would always try to follow His requirements and be hot and on fire for the word of God.

I assure you, being on fire for the wonderful word of God illustrates our best eternity option. Because our Great Creator God will remember all hot and on fire Christians when they present themselves before Him, I am certain He'll be proud to claim all hot and on fire Christians as His children.

CHAPTER TWENTY-FOUR

THE REASON MY STORY WRITING CAREER IS ONGOING

Indeed, my story writing career is ongoing and hasn't a finish date because I am hopelessly in love with the word of God, and I can't foresee a stopping point on my own accord. As long as my mind is clear and my connection to God is strong, I'll continue writing Bible-related stories.

The word of God goes through my mind all the time, regardless of whether I am asleep or awake. I am proud to say that the word of God is much more exciting than watching a television movie. Indeed, I am glad to say I cannot get enough of the gospel of God.

The word of God consumes my thoughts throughout the day, and I rise in the early morning hours to give my heart to the wonderful word of God. I am unmarried, yet I am married, and because of my great love for the word of God, I happily conclude I am married to the gospel of God.

Simply because the life-saving gospel of God is my great love, and I eat it, drink it, and love every word of God. I sincerely believe His scriptures and miracles are true, and He has a place prepared for you and me. Furthermore, the Son of God tells His apostles He goes away to prepare a place for them and everyone who loves Him.

My heart desires to attend the marriage feast of the Lamb and become a member of His wonderful family. At the wedding feast, I want to witness the bond of love between the bride and the bridegroom firsthand.

Indeed, being in love with a mate is one thing, but being in love with a dream from above and a righteous way of life is another. Because of the gospel He represents, I am in love with the word of God, and the desires of my heart are married to His perfect ways of life.

The beautiful Ten Commandments of God are my wedding ring, and the wonderful bridegroom is my King, and I am strongly entwined to both of them. My world revolves around them; they are the centerpiece of my life, and living without the guidance of the Ten Commandments would be like living without a heart.

I proudly tell you I am hopelessly bound by an invisible and unbreakable chain to His covenant words, and the bond cannot be seen with the naked eye. But just the same, the chain between us is unbreakable, and I cannot resist the urge to follow after Him.

The unbreakable chain between my Creator God and me is made from the substance of love, and love is the strongest and the most unbreakable chain of all chains, even though love cannot be seen with the naked eye. But if I could calculate, I am sure my love for my Creator is bigger than the universe.

Positively, I would be lost without having the unbreakable chain of love between God and me, and there's nothing better than being loved by God. Proudly, I testify that the intangible substance of love is more valuable than the tangible substance of silver and gold.

I advise you to love the wonderful word of God and be married to His righteous ways. If you are dedicated to Him, I am sure He'll prepare a mansion in His kingdom for you and allow you to cruise above the clouds for eternity.

CHAPTER TWENTY-FIVE

MY ODYSSEY

I am the sole writer and creative story designer of nine published books, and for the benefit of higher learning, they consist of five hundred and twenty-nine individual bible stories. Because the Potter Man in Heaven directs my thoughts, they are rare and unique stories not many writers will write about.

However, I've written another twenty-three books, amounting to over one million and five hundred thousand words. And all together, they have one thousand individual stories. But they aren't ready yet, and it will take me a while to get them ready.

I assure you, no one else is privileged to do any writing for me, and I wouldn't want anyone else to write my stories. I am glad to say all my stories are created from my studies and thoughts, and I am quite certain my inspiration person is the beautiful Holy Ghost of God.

Too many times, famous and rich people want a book to call their own, and they hire someone to do their writing for them, then they call the finished work their work. But it doesn't seem right, or exactly correct, to call a book your own if someone else writes it for you.

Especially if the hired writer uses their designed words to portray the book's contents and writes a style different from the storyteller's before we can honestly claim total ownership. I'll always believe the author must express the analogies and events in his own words before he can be called the writer.

Indeed, the thoughts and words being expressed aren't the full expressions of the man who hires someone else to do his writing for him. Truly, I am trying to say that every word being expressed needs to be expressed by the person calling himself the author of his book.

Furthermore, I want you to know it takes a lot of words to create a book, and if you give someone else information, you let them express it in their words and from their point of view; then I ask you, who is the author? Is it the person expressing the story who relays the information in the book, and can the person revealing the story to a hired author call it their book?

Indeed, it seems to be cheating if we let someone else express our words for us and write our story in a manner different from our own. If we make this compromise, I believe the author's personality will be mixed with the writer's thoughts and choice of words.

I suppose everyone has a different point of view concerning what's right and wrong and acceptable and unacceptable. However, I have to say a hired writer cannot express our words as accurately as we can express the meaning and portrayal of the subject being written.

Indeed, many people hire a professional writer and let him write them an eloquent book, and it appears that the person doing the hiring is the eloquent writer since it's their name on the book. However, the only accurate word able to describe such doings is deception.

Simply because we must be the writer before the book can portray our expressions, and using another person's skills means it's wrong if we put our name on a literary work someone else wrote for us. But this sort of thing always happens, even if someone other than the author writes the book.

Furthermore, how can anyone receive satisfaction and feel good about a finished work if they put their name on someone else's writing? Especially when the storyteller knows it's someone else's interpretation of our expression being written.

I want you to know that these rare and unusual books and all the Bible stories I write are my words only, and they are my exciting journey and my odyssey through the excellent word of God. I assure you every word written in my books accurately represents my story and style and not someone else's.

These revealing books and all the Bible stories I write are my accomplishments against the powers of darkness and the evil spirit god of this world. I have much to say about these seriously important subjects in my book, and I want them fully told to enhance understanding.

Furthermore, I assure you, because Satan is a fearsome warrior against Bible knowledge, it takes a strong determination to write the Bible stories I write, and only a few people will ever succeed. The prince of darkness, who rules this world, is against the Bible stories I write, and he opposes me and my love for God.

This truth means the demon spirits of the air are the same devils guilty of opposing God in Heaven, and during the first earth age, before the great cleansing flood, they have the power of telepathy and know who their enemy is in the flesh. Truly, I assure you they oppose anyone, during any Earth age, who does the works of God.

Furthermore, the perfect ways of God and the prize of immortality are the most important gifts we can secure on this Earth. But since the righteous ways of God and the prize of immortality aren't given much consideration by most people living on this Earth.

It proves the spirits of the air, who have the power of telepathy, will stop many good teachings from being accomplished on this Earth. I assure you, these demonic spirits successfully steer many people away from the perfect ways of God and the grand prize of immortality.

Therefore, as I do, important works are meant to spread the gospel of God on the highways and byways and to everyone interested. It's a hard task for any person to accomplish, and it's a battle against demon spirits only a few men will overcome and make a difference.

Simply because, for one reason or another, most Christians cannot overcome the demon spirits of the air and their most powerful weapon, called the power of telepathy. Sadly, because of the power of telepathy, men and women cannot fulfill the need in this world to increase Bible knowledge. Proudly, I guarantee the works I do to enhance the gospel of God anger the demonic spirits of the air.

Indeed, with the help of the wonderful Holy Ghost, I've managed to resist the demon spirits of the air and their anti-godly power of telepathy. Truly, because my living temple is clean and I fight against their influence, I can give this world these extremely unusual Bible stories.

I assure you, my God-inspired Odyssey isn't different from the Odyssey of Odysseus, who struggled against the gods of the sea, the air, and the underworld spirits. Except for the fact my odyssey is real and not fiction, and it has a holy purpose to accomplish.

Furthermore, a movie is for entertainment, and I guarantee that my Odyssey is much more important to mankind than the fictional Odyssey of Odysseus. Indeed, this is my destiny, and my stories are not for entertainment but are written to save souls. Maybe the stories I write are why I am here and now at this particular timeline in the history of mankind.

However, whether this is my destiny or not, my struggle against the wicked prince of this world ends when my spirit separates from the flesh. When it's over, I hope to go home with the blessings of my Father, Yehovah, and I will be proud to stand before God and say; I've tried to complement your works.

Positively, until my going home day comes, I'll not change what I am doing, and I'll continue to wrestle against principalities, evil powers, and spiritual wickedness in high places. Because I love the God of creation and His Ten Commandments, I will live the rest of my life trying to teach men about God.

Furthermore, when I leave this world, I will travel onward to be with my wonderful Creator God. I want you to know that the work I leave behind will be my testimony, and my works will prove I stood strong for the word of God and fought against the evil prince of the air.

I want you to realize because you'll fight spiritual battles, too, the wicked prince of the air is the ghost god of this world. The wicked ghost god is Lucifer, the evil and devious Serpent of Old, who was physically here on this Earth before the great cleansing flood.

In my books, these extremely unusual and one-of-a-kind stories are meant to teach and expose many important subjects to believers in Christ. I can sincerely say that my type of stories reveals why I've been chosen to write Bible stories uniquely different from mainstream stories.

The unusual and serious Bible stories I write break the boundaries between light and darkness, Bible illiteracy, great knowledge, and spiritual blindness; maybe, because of my effort, some people will be inspired to love God and live by His commanded ways forever.

Many of my Bible stories differ from regular mainstream stories; they venture into the unknown realms. But my odyssey and my ongoing battle against the evil ghost spirits of this world isn't anything new, not since the great flood receded four thousand years ago.

Positively, my odyssey is nearly the same, or at the least, similar to the same odyssey, and the same battle every professing Christian fights to win the prize of immortality. I want you to know we must be loyal and dedicated to the word of God before we can be effective warriors for God.

Indeed, I advise you to fight the hounds of Hell and not let them take your soul through trickery and deception. Mainly because a child of God will receive good rewards for fighting against the demons from Hell, but a child of Lucifer will receive damnation and a free ride to the pits of Hell.

Conclusively, I assure you that receiving the gift of immortality is better than death in the fire, and I ask you, who can debate with this analogy? Please know the Bible scriptures are clear, and after our last breath, we go up or down from here.

The generations before us prove our time runs out sooner than we think, and regardless of what we are, here and now, after the death of the flesh comes judgment, and only the God lovers will win the prize of immortality.

For the above reason, all my Bible-related stories are easy to read, and I sincerely testify the above reason explains the importance of my stories to this world. Truly, if I had one wish for this world, it would be granted.

Then I would ask my wonderful Supernatural God, please instill the desire to be Bible-savvy into everyone's heart. After that, this world would be better, and Bible illiteracy couldn't be the reason for a world entangled in sin.

The excellent and wonderful King James Bible, inspired by my Great Creator God, consists of approximately 780,000 words, and all of us are judged from three words written within it. I assure you there will come a day and a time when these three words will exceed the importance of all other words.

The three determining words are as important as the air we breathe, and the temperature of the heart, hot, cold, and lukewarm, judges all of us. Urgently, I warn you, hot better be our temperature when we meet our Great Creator God face to face on Judgment Day.

Beyond the shadow of a doubt, God will reject the cold and the lukewarm person, and they will not be allowed into His peaceful kingdom. For this reason, I urge you to be hot and on fire for the beautiful word of God and not let your fire go out.

However, observation proves this is mostly an ungodly world, and most people do not give much thought or adhere to God's required word. Sadly, I must tell you, the excellent gift of salvation will elude a great unknown number of cold and lukewarm people in this world.

Therefore, my analogy indicates that this world is in trouble with our Great Creator God, and it's because of opposition to His required word. I warn you so you can change your wicked ways, and if we oppose Him, we will have trouble with Him.

Our beautiful Ten Commandments of God reveal this troubled world is going in the wrong direction. This observation makes my Bible stories much more important than men and women realize because men perish for lack of Bible knowledge.

However, I want you to know this problem can be solved by studying our great Bible and getting to know God. I advise you to love God as I do and try to educate the unlearned before they perish from a lack of bible knowledge.

I assure you, if our heart is godly, and the word of God is meaningful to us, then we are our brother's keeper to an unknown degree, but not an enabler. Surely, the unknown degree should, at least, include us caring about our brother's salvation.

Deliverance from sin and the gift of salvation isn't the information we should withhold from anyone looking for our Savior God. Furthermore, not caring about salvation for our neighbors, children, brothers, and sisters is cruel.

Truly, Christ-like behavior means we Christians should desire everyone to win the prize of immortality. Being Christ-like means we should rejoice like the angels in Heaven do when a sinner finds God and converts to Christianity.

CHAPTER TWENTY-SIX

MY INSPIRATION

I am not Catholic, nor am I Protestant, Baptist, or Muslim, and I do not pattern myself by going to any certain kind of church building. I have no denomination, nor do manmade church rules bind me, but I am a pure, unwavering Christian and full of love for God and His word.

I belong to God's living church. Yeshua is my inspiration, and I love all the great godliness He supports. The church I belong to walks and talks, and it spreads the gospel of God into all four corners of this Earth, and the quality of it dives into His word as deep as we want to dive.

The theology of theologians does not spoil me, and I haven't conformed to all of their philosophies, nor do I agree with them. My great inspirational teacher is the Holy Ghost, who lives within me and guides my thoughts.

For the above reason, I can write the greatest collection of Bible stories ever written by any man, past or present. I write these unusual books and the Bible stories I reveal to the people in this world because I believe it's my destiny to do so since birth.

Positively, the evil prince of this world became my arch-enemy early in life, and three unusual things happened to me in my youth. I believe they prove that Satan was trying to destroy my life way before I could write the Bible-related stories I write.

I assure you, the wicked Satan has set many traps and snares before me throughout my lifetime, and I am certain he was trying to stop me from accomplishing my Bible-related work. But thanks to God and His wonderful mercy, I am still alive, even though my being alive defies the odds.

Therefore, I have to believe I am alive for a good reason and to make a significant difference in this world. For this reason, I dedicate and proclaim my works are written to benefit higher learning and win souls to Christ.

I also know that the knowledge my Bible stories are written with comes from God, and it's His perfect word; all my writing entwines with mainly because I could not write my stories without having the excellent and special Holy Ghost sharing His wisdom with me.

Therefore, the writing I do with the pen and pencil is the work of the Potter Man, who shaped me into what I am today. I assure you, the Potter Man shapes many vessels made out of clay, and you and I are a form of clay. But without a doubt, we are an unfinished project.

God knew you and me from the foundation of this Earth, and it was way before we came forth from our mother's womb. This truth means I am a burning star from the Ancient of Days, and I have work to do for God as Samson, Moses, and Elijah did before my soul exits this Earth.

The good angels protect me so I can complete a finished work never before achieved by any man. I assure you, my Bible-related work is specifically written for the lifting of God's odyssey on this Earth, and someday, His odyssey will create a perfect society.

Indeed, suppose you and I have gladly submitted our will to God, regardless of the age at which our conversion to Christianity began. In that case, our odyssey is entwined with God's, and He will improve the clay shaping of every individual seeking to be His helping friend.

These three events happening in my youth, I've mentioned, could be supernatural in origin, and I believe the supernatural was involved in these three events. I want you to know that the devil also knows our thoughts and hates whoever loves God. Truly, I don't doubt he hates me and will be my enemy until my soul departs from my flesh.

My long and furious battle against the devil's wiles and his terrible influence has prodded me to be a thorn in his side and resulted in the greatest collection of Bible stories ever written by any man since the beginning of time.

This personal story, portraying me as the clay, is called my inspiration. It's entwined with the Potter Man's inspiration since the new me loves the Potter Man, and I desire to do His work. I declare that believers in Christ are developed whenever we despise ungodliness, and the clay shapes the right way.

This informative story has a dual meaning, and it's meant to be your inspiration, too, since you are also entwined with our wonderful God. I want you to know our Great Creator God loves a loyal Christian, and He expects you and me to do good things for His glory.

Therefore, clean up your living temple, let the Holy Ghost be your teacher, and learn all you can about my wonderful God. Then fulfill your odyssey, entwined with God's because He's your inspiration and your Potter Man.

CHAPTER TWENTY-SEVEN

MY ADVICE TO BIBLE STORY WRITERS

This personal story reveals the advice I would offer anyone who desires to write Bible stories and advance the gospel of God. I would warn them and say, be prepared to fight with the evil spirits of the air because they will fight you much harder than they fight with most men.

If you write Bible stories, you are one among the few, and I guarantee you'll be the target of severe attacks from every avenue of darkness. The evil spirits of the air and ungodly men influenced by them will make it a point to oppose you, and you may as well realize you have an enemy for life, and your spiritual war will increase.

I would say stick to the Bible and not take on other men's philosophies, especially if they are assumption philosophies. Be wise, and do not write your stories based on the traditions of men because my Great God of Heaven and Earth hates the traditions of men.

The Son of God tells us because He wants us to know, the traditions of men make the perfect word of God of no effect. For this reason, do not include the traditions of men in any of your writing unless you expose the traditions of men as opposed to the commanded word of God.

I want you to know that men's traditions are the thoughts and writing of men, and sometimes, men will try to replace God's word with men's traditions. I assure you that exposing the traditions of men is commendable and needs to be done by more loyal men of God.

I would tell you to study your Bible intensely and keep your living temple clean, and the Holy Ghost will be strong in you. Furthermore, I want you to know you cannot write good Bible stories unless you have help from the Holy Ghost, and He does want to help you.

However, please realize He will not live inside an unclean temple; unclean Christians cannot force Him to dwell in their hearts. For this reason, you'll not write great and unusual Bible stories unless you are determined to keep a clean-living temple.

I want you to remember the living temple of the wonderful Holy Ghost is your heart, and the cleaner your heart, the more mysteries and puzzles He'll reveal during your daily walk with Him. Because you desire to be godly and have a voice crying out in the wilderness of this world, you need to know all you can learn about my Great God.

Unlearned men perish for lack of Bible knowledge, but you should choose to be extremely Bible-savvy. If you are determined to make yourself extremely wise in the word of God, you will write good Bible stories and win the great prize of immortality.

Indeed, only a few people in this Lucifer-controlled world are called to write Bible stories seriously, especially the strong meat of Christianity. Sadly, most Christians who write a religious or a Christian-based story usually avoid the strong meat of Christianity.

Most Christian authors will choose to write an inspirational story, which usually involves themselves or something they've witnessed. But my Bible stories are mostly the meat of Christianity, filled with important information about God and His terrible adversary, Lucifer.

My stories are impartial, and race, color, or gender is irrelevant to me as it is to God. My Bible-related stories coincide with the commanded word of God, and they cut whoever falls under the sword of the Lord and lift whoever knocks on His door.

My advice to anyone wanting to write Bible stories is to do it passionately, with strong courage and boldness, and tell the required word of God exactly as it's written. Don't beat around the bush, but be a straight shooter, and do not be afraid to put a definition to sin.

Furthermore, write your Bible stories enthusiastically and passionately because the word of God isn't passive. Nor are the Father, the Son, and the Holy Ghost passive. Use John the Baptist as an example of strong character because it's a tragic shame to be passive concerning the needed word of God.

Positively, concerning the subject being explored, add as much detail as you can to every Bible-related story you write and explain it in the simplest terms so that everyone can understand the subject's meaning.

Furthermore, before you can succeed at writing unique Bible stories, you will have to be hot and on fire for the wonderful word of God. I assure you that being a hot and on-fire Christian is glorious and makes the heart feel good, and I testify to this hot and on-fire statement.

This personal story, *My Advice To Bible Story Writers,* personifies me, and I assure you, I've learned everything I've told you the hard way. But nothing else in this world has pleased me more than learning about my beautiful God and teaching His word to the unlearned.

I love my Great Creator God and all of His commanded ways, and I hope you passionately do too; if you do, it will make your heart feel good. Before this inspirational story ends, I want you to know that the word of God is the ultimate pinnacle of everything holy, clean, and good.

CHAPTER TWENTY-EIGHT

FOLLOW HIM OR DENY HIM

This extremely serious story, *Follow Him Or Deny Him*, has a required meaning and cannot be completed by one party. This truth means it'll take an agreement from both parties to be valid because *Following Him Or Denying Him* has to be mutually agreed to before a covenant is formed.

The subject concerning all of us: Following Him Or Denying Him refers to the righteous world of God, and following or denying is every person's choice. Following Him Or Denying Him began in Heaven with the angels, and they had free will to follow or deny our Great Creator God. This realization means they had free will and could choose between right and wrong.

Indeed, we flesh and blood people on this Earth have the same free will as all the rebellious angels in Heaven. This truth means we can follow or deny God with the same freedom, and the enormous population on this Earth illustrates a split in what men and women do.

The word serve doesn't mean we are puppets to a Master or a tyrant God who doesn't allow freedom. But the word serve in this story means we are servants to a righteous way of life, only our Great Creator God provides.

Anyway, I assure you, our Creator God isn't a tyrant God and doesn't want to make servant puppets out of every person in His kingdom. Although, He is looking for men and women in love with righteousness, who are willing to be servants of righteousness for eternity.

The word denies in this explanation story refers to men and women who gladly reject being servants to righteousness. In all fairness, the excellent gift of free will allows every person living in the flesh the privilege to accept Him as their God or to deny Him.

Although I want you to know our choice to Follow Him Or Deny Him must be made while we live on this Earth. This truth means we have a limited time to make up our minds and to decide whether or not we want to be a child of God in love with His commandments.

I want you to realize after the death of the flesh, our ability to follow Him or refuse Him is set in concrete, and being set in concrete means a different choice or direction in life cannot be chosen after the death of our flesh. For this reason, I hope you realize at the end of our life, we go up, or sadly, we go down.

However, the truth is certain after men and women realize the Son of God is our Mediator between His Father and us. Then, all ungodly people who traveled the wide road and went down to the kingdom of Satan will be remorseful and wish they hadn't rejected Him.

Especially when ungodly people discover rejection of our Great Creator God means damnation and eventually smoke and ashes, and the final equation means we'll either receive a spiritual body or become smoke and ashes. Sadly, some men and women never see the light and walk on the narrow road, but they believe in a lie and are damned.

However, I want you to know my wonderful God is a merciful God, and being a merciful God means He'll forgive sinners if they repent for their sins and change into a servant of righteousness. But please realize being merciful doesn't mean He'll allow wicked men into His kingdom; that wouldn't repent and change.

Therefore, the option to repent and change must be sought after and achieved while we are alive, and it would be extremely wise for sinners to submit themselves to the ways of the Lord before their option to change and become Christ-like disappears.

I also assure you that being alive tomorrow shouldn't be assumed because death can come unexpectedly and suddenly sometimes. Even when men think they have a long life ahead of them. But the truth is reality and as mysterious as the wind, and our life is compared to a vapor, and gambling on a vapor is a bad gamble.

Our excellent and wonderful bible is filled with the perfect word of our Great Creator God. His word is designed to care about our lives, and His gospel reveals many important things for our benefit. However, I hope you realize we must discover, remember, and utilize His commanded word before it's beneficial.

Indeed, our God-inspired Bible reveals we are standing in the middle ground right now between Heaven and Hell. But after the death of our flesh, Heaven or Hell will become one of our destination places. This truth means life doesn't end at the grave, and it doesn't have to end at all.

Therefore, I want you to realize choices matter, and you should be concerned about your soul's destiny. Every day anyone puts off giving themselves to the Lord illustrates a gamble with salvation and a long life of immortality, and I must say, it's foolish to be a gambler on eternal life.

Indeed, the only logical and wise decision before it's too late is not to wait another day to be a child of God. Deciding to be a child of God is an important decision no one will regret, and gladness of the heart should be the emotion we feel for converting to Christianity.

Anyway, I am telling you, the change from a sinner person to the conversion of a Christian is an improvement in anyone's life. The change from a sinner to a God lover reveals the formula for designing a better person, and the definition of a better person is a commandment lover faithful to God.

Indeed, regardless of our previous lifestyle and mistakes during our rebellious moments in our youth. I want you to realize that my wonderful and merciful God will allow us to pick up the cross and follow Him if our hearts are sincere concerning repentance and change.

I assure you that obedience to the righteous word of God illustrates our proof of change, and we need to prove ourselves changed. But on the other hand, rebellion against the righteous word of God illustrates proof of rejection and our refusal to change.

Furthermore, any person not interested in picking up the cross and carrying the gospel of God wherever they go. Then, they aren't worthy of being called the sons and daughters of God, nor are they worthy to live in His peaceful kingdom after the death of their flesh.

Furthermore, the unchanged person will never know about the wonderful gifts my Great God has in store for whoever loves Him. But the choice to follow or deny Him is our decision, and because He believes in free will, He'll not interfere with our choice.

The wise decision is clear: do not wait too long to choose the God of salvation, and mainly because, sometimes, we leave this world suddenly. Sometimes, we leave this world without having time for deathbed repentance and conversion to Christianity.

This informative story, *Following Him Or Denying Him*, describes me and the important option I faced at a critical time. This personal story reveals me as a sinner until I followed Him instead of denying Him.

I assure you, choosing to follow Him has been the wisest decision I've ever made, and I haven't any intentions of looking back. I am certain plenty of people stand at the crossroads in life and are faced with the decision to follow or deny their one and only Savior.

I hope this personal story I've written to everyone helps me and many other people similar to me, and I hope it inspires men and women to follow Him instead of denying Him. But please be aware that rejecting Him is the same as rejecting an everlasting life of immortality.

CHAPTER TWENTY-NINE

THE VANITY CONTEST

In this close-to-the-heart story, you and I see demonstrated in real life quite often; it revolves around a contest of vanity. As much as I wish it weren't true, this sad story portrays an ongoing contest between our appearance and the constantly aging flesh.

Indeed, the corridor of time proves that the constantly aging flesh has the advantage of beauty. Because it's a natural way to think, the eyes of men and women prefer a beautiful image much more than they prefer wrinkles and gray hair or no hair at all.

However, I am certain you already know every day, our age increases, and day after day, time destroys beauty much quicker than time destroys the flesh. Truly, during our golden years, age is a heavy weight on vanity, and we aren't so beautiful when we look in the mirror.

Even though the constantly aging flesh has a limited lifespan, it'll still outlast the lifespan of a beautiful appearance if we live to a ripe old age. Indeed, vanity is a useless way to feel because the natural order of things reveals the assets attached to beauty are short-term and only last a few years.

Beyond the shadow of a doubt, it defies logic and good judgment, but beauty always receives the most attention, even if undeserved. Surely, you and I are foolish men and women if we allow the beauty of flesh to receive more attention than good judgment.

I assure you, most everything created under the sun looks more beautiful when it's young and new and has less wear and tear. But wear and tear add up, year after year, and age deteriorates beauty if it's made of flesh.

I believe the Father, the Son, and the Holy Ghost didn't allow us pictures of them because they want us to realize our image on the outside of our bones isn't as important as the image of our inner character. Our character is of monumental importance, and the Ten Commandments build the right character, and not abiding by them creates character flaws.

I assure you, it's vain to believe the image of our flesh will always be beautiful, even if we are beautiful in our youth, because the beauty of youth disappears with age, and no one can defeat the progression of age or change its results.

This truth means beauty doesn't last too long before old age replaces it with wrinkles and scars. Although I wish all men were handsome and never grew old, just as I wish all women were beautiful forever. As for me, my lady is seventy years of age, and her beauty never fades away.

However, the fact remains clear and reality is our mirror, and it's quite obvious God designed our life cycle to deteriorate with age, and we cannot alter the results of age. Truly, if we look into the mirror, we can see ourselves growing older each day and watch our beauty fade away.

Positively, this analogy is as predictable as saying the sun comes up every morning and goes down every evening. And it's a good thing for us; our outward beauty doesn't judge us. Because in the end, we'd have hell to pay after much wear and tear.

Truly, it's a good thing for us; the beauty of our hearts is the barometer God reads because the heart and the beauty of the flesh do not always speak the same language. I declare beauty is fragile like glass, not as enduring as grass, and not durable like a good heart.

Sadly, the conclusion to the matter concerning beauty reveals that appearance is a contest between our character and flesh. This truth means our appearance is the reason for many decisions, and our appearance shouldn't be our decision-maker.

I guarantee that reading romance novels and looking at ourselves in the mirror isn't the formula for a beautiful heart. I want you to know the God of creation isn't impressed by beautiful flesh, and the beautiful Queen of Sheba found out that charm and beauty don't influence God.

However, reading romance novels and constantly looking into the mirror indicates a vain character, and a vain character is a formula for ungodliness, adultery, and all sorts of immoral and carnal sins. Sadly, vanity is a runaway train, and neighbors worldwide are having a vanity contest.

Indeed, old age gets the last say, and popularity decreases as our beauty fades away. This truth means youth and beautiful looks symbolize flowers blooming in the spring but fading away and dying in the fall. Surely, the parallel between nature and man is a preview of the flesh, only we aren't perennials.

Indeed, too much emphasis is put on beauty rather than godliness and the seriousness of being Christ-like. But the Creator of man is the giver and taker of life, and because of His design, godliness will increase your longevity in the next life and much more than the advantages of beauty.

I am certain the final results at the end of our life will prove good character is worth much more than beautiful flesh, and what more value can a person achieve in life than being beautiful, godly, and good-hearted? God bless you beautiful people with beautiful hearts and a Christ-like character, and may all your days be happy.

Furthermore, whoever you are, never forget to cherish your beautiful heart because it's an everlasting treasure, more valuable than beautiful flesh. Always remember a beautiful heart will cause a person less trouble than beautiful flesh.

For a true example given to us from the Heavens above, we shouldn't ever forget. The evil and rebellious Lucifer, as spectacular as a sapphire diamond glittering in the light, was lifted because of his beautiful appearance. But Lucifer had a troubled life because of self-imposed vanity; undoubtedly, vanity contributed to his foolish imagination, and he fell from Heaven like a falling star.

It's for the above reason and because of his beautiful appearance; his image was his greatest obstacle in life. This truth means a beautiful appearance has a great amount of influence on carnal and immoral opportunities and the way we proceed through life.

However, the fact remains true and unchallengeable, too. A beautiful heart is the best and is much more valuable than the appearance of beautiful flesh. Surely, when the votes come in, the flesh doesn't stand a chance in a long-term vanity contest.

CONDITIONAL OR UNCONDITIONAL

Concerning the divine promises of our wonderful God, many preachers and teachers are divided on the formula for receiving them. Truly, it's easy to conclude that the formula for receiving divine promises is controversial among Christian preachers and churches.

Some preachers say divine promises are conditional, and some say they aren't conditional, and this difference of opinion alone illustrates an example of divided opinions among Christians. Indeed, I want you to know this story will reveal the conditional and the unconditional.

Positively, this informative story is called *Conditional Or Unconditional*, and it revolves around whether or not we can claim the promises of God. However, before this story starts, I want you to know not all Christians are positioned right to claim the promises of God.

For this reason, this awareness story will put a conclusion to the meaning of conditional or unconditional promises. This true conclusion is a need to understand the subject, and it's revealed for our benefit. Undoubtedly, we will be wiser believers in Christ by knowing the conditional and the unconditional.

Indeed, throughout our Bible, God makes several promises and agreements to professing Christians who meet His requirements. Some of His promises are conditional, and some are unconditional, and one shouldn't be confused with the other.

However, I tell you, no man, nor any woman, can be sinful, wicked, sensual, and immoral and still be able to claim God's promises even if they are a professing Christian because sin will separate us from the promises of God, regardless of our religious proclamation.

Therefore, the conclusion is undiscriminating, which means most of God's promises are conditional. This truth means that not all sons and daughters of God can claim the same promises of God. After knowing this truth, I must tell you the God of Heaven and Earth usually expects something in return for giving away divine promises.

Especially if someone is expecting divine promises that don't meet certain conditions about the promise of God, and this means God doesn't give away all His promises free of charge. Truly, we would be foolish to believe all Christians are equally positioned to claim His promises.

The next informative scripture is a warning, and my wonderful and wise God is speaking words of wisdom through the Apostle Paul. The Apostle Paul tells us that we must be separated from the ungodliness in this world before our Great God will receive us as sons and daughters.

2 Corinthians 6:17 Wherefore, come out from among <u>them</u>, (The children of the world, who follow the rebellious ways of Lucifer, and who so ever practices any form of paganism),

2 Corinthians 6:17 and be ye <u>separate</u> (means separate ourselves from the commandments of men and the traditions of men,

Furthermore, we may have to separate ourselves from the Sun-day churches and any temple building, where paganism and Christianity are mixed and wherever pure and authentic Christianity is defiled. I assure you that defiling the word of God is the major reason divine promises are hard to receive.

2 Corinthians 6:17 said the Lord, and touch not the <u>unclean</u> (means touch not the unfit, and touch not the unholy, whether they are man or beast), and <u>I</u> (God) will receive you.

Indeed, the above promise is conditional and can only be claimed by any Christian if certain conditions are adhered to for receiving the promise. Adhered to means, God commands all men and women who profess to be Christians to be clean and separated people.

The definition of separated people has many meanings, but it's written literally and not symbolically, and it must be taken at face value. Since the Holy Ghost of God desires to live within us, we must keep Him a clean dwelling place, or He'll not live inside our hearts.

If we want to be loyal sons or daughters to God, the honest person must be separated from the corrupt and the holy from the unholy. This accomplishment is achieved through our actions and talk, and not abiding by His commandments means we'll not receive divine promises.

The clean must be separated from the unclean, and all professing Christians must be separated from any form of paganism because the converted people of God are commanded to be different from the wicked, corrupt, and unclean children of this world.

However, I want you to understand a professing Christian can stray from the right way and fit into this world, belonging to the ungodly. But if they are a commandment keeper, they cannot be a part of the world of the ungodly and be commandment breakers and do ungodly things and receive divine promises.

However, if you and I are faithful and separate from the ungodly and unclean things in this world, our God of Judgment will be a Father to you and me, and we shall be sons and daughters to Him. I am sure our next life will be in His kingdom because we do His will.

Therefore, most of the promises of God are usually conditional because everyone has a backsliding possibility. For this reason, He doesn't say all His promises are unconditional, and saying all His promises are unconditional amounts to a false statement. Truly, you and I are foolish to believe we can compromise His word and receive His promises.

Indeed, we would be foolish to believe the stipulated requirements of God don't bind us, and saying all His promises are unconditional is misleading and a hurtful lie, especially if we are unlearned Christians, depending on the truth taught from the pulpit.

Indeed, it can be a big letdown for many unlearned Christians who do not see their prayer requests answered and do not know why the God of creation isn't answering. It could be because they've been taught the promises of God are unconditional, and they wrongly believe nothing is required from them except to believe in Him.

Usually, these same preachers, who preach and teach unconditional standards, are not bound by God-given requirements. They are the same preachers who will say your sins are forgiven, past, present, and future, including the ones you haven't committed yet.

All I can say concerning this fabricated philosophy is they preach and teach their opinion. But I want you to know opinions and assumptions aren't always the accurate word of God. Sadly, I must tell you, the unlearned person assumes inaccuracies.

However, if you read the word of God and apply your heart to learning the scriptures, then, for your well-being, you'll not be overtaken by myths and false beliefs. You'll be able to know the promises of God are usually conditional, and they usually have stipulated requirements attached to receiving the promises of God.

Most of the time, when our supernatural God makes a promise, He'll usually say, If you'll do as I say, if you'll be a separated people, or if you'll keep My commandments. Truly, you must know that He doesn't kid around concerning His stipulation requirements.

I assure you, the little word called *if* makes His promises conditional. Otherwise, God wouldn't use the little word called *if* in conjunction with His promises. The word called *if* amounts to an ever-expanding word, saying if you'll resist the unclean, and resist the unfit, and the unholy.

Then, you can be a son or a daughter to God, and this statement sounds pretty conditional. The words spoken within the scripture in Second Corinthians 6:17 should be taken seriously and not forgotten.

The scripture says God will receive us when we separate ourselves from the corrupt children of this world and when we refuse to touch the unclean. After knowing this truth, it would be foolish to believe everything God has to offer Christians is given away unconditionally.

Lucifer is the evil, rebellious angel from Heaven who aims to harm Christianity, and I conclude he's the mastermind behind the boldest and the most terrible robbery in the history of Christianity.

This truth means his robbery proves Lucifer's goal is to destroy God's promises and keep them from helping needy Christians. For this reason, I'll call Lucifer the destroyer of Christianity and the destroyer of God-made promises.

Positively, Lucifer is a wicked manipulator, and he causes men and women to make the word of God of no effect. Lucifer is the evil prince of this world, guilty of casting stumbling blocks in the pathway of the promises of God.

I assure you the perverted and evil things of this world are okay with Lucifer, but God's perfect and righteous ways aren't okay with Lucifer. Truly, the vision of unconditional promises is an imaginary dream unless we try to keep the commandments of God.

Indeed, do not be so unlearned you'll naively believe whatever you ask for you'll receive just because you are a professing Christian. Mainly because most of the promises of God aren't unconditional, and we cannot receive them because we ask for them.

This truth means most divine promises must be earned through the stipulations of His commandments, and I assure you, nothing is gained without a fight. The ways of Lucifer are our adversary between God and us and claiming His divine promises.

Indeed, choosing to follow the Ten Commandments of God illustrates the only formula for claiming the promises of God, and rebellion against the Ten Commandments falls under the same guidelines as the definition of the little word called *if*.

Furthermore, most of the promises of our Great God hinge on the extremely important and serious word called *if* and if you and I leave the little word called *if* out of the formula for claiming the wonderful promises of God.

Then, we'll never understand what's conditional and what's unconditional, according to the required word of God. Indeed, it's sad for a Christian to spend many years in the church and not know what's conditional and unconditional.

I gladly wittness the word of God isn't grievous if we love it, but the word of God is grievous if we are living differently or other than His required ways. This truth means the helpful promises of God will be easier to claim if we are hopelessly in love with His word.

Conclusively, the promises of God aren't an automatic giveaway because we've converted to Christianity, and it's because the word *if* requires a code of standards. However, if I were going to claim a promise made by God, I would entwine my lifestyle to His stipulations and not look for automatic giveaways.

CHAPTER THIRTY-ONE

NATURE CONTRASTS WITH MEN

In many ways, nature teaches mankind the structure of reality if we are willing to learn the signs attached to the order of things. The reality of nature never changes from generation to generation, and the natural order of things continues year after year. Certainly, it's been this way since the creation of Adam and Eve, and nothing will change until the last days.

I assure you great wisdom can be learned by observing the nature of unchangeable things. But who am I but a simple man, and how can I know such wisdom, except I learn it from an exceptional God-inspired prophet?

Therefore, and for the benefit of higher learning, I'll turn this story over to a privileged man with great wisdom. As recorded in our Bible, he's called the great preacher man, and his wisdom exceeds the boundaries of the normal and average person.

This declaration story concerns you, right and wrong, and me. The great preacher uses nature and man's works to express what is necessary and expose the meaning of vanity and vexation. I want you to know the works of his hands taught the great preacher man much of his wisdom.

The sun ariseth, and the sun goeth down, and day after day, it hasteth back to the same place where it arose. Therefore, the great preacher man was blessed with much wisdom, and he reveals the reality of nature, and it entwines with the reality of man, and he speaks.

The wind goeth toward the south and turneth about unto the north, and it whirleth about continually, and then it returneth again to its circuits. All the rivers run into the sea, yet the sea is not full, and into the place from where the rivers come, there shall they return.

The things that have been are that which shall be, and that which is done are that which shall be done. This truth means there aren't new things of nature under the sun, and the God-designed order of nature continues year after year.

Therefore, I ask you, is there anything of nature, of which it may be said, see this is new? However, nothing is new under the sun; it has already been of old times before us. Surely, through his assessment the great preacher man says our Creator God has given a circuit to everything.

Ecclesiastes 1:11 There is no remembrance of former things; neither shall there be a remembrance of things to come with those that shall come after.

Ecclesiastes 1:14 (And the great preacher man says), I have seen <u>all</u> <u>the</u> <u>works</u> (of man) that are done under the sun; and; behold, <u>all</u> (the works of man) is <u>vanity</u> (means worthless, futile, and mostly unimportant),

Ecclesiastes 1:14 and <u>vexation</u> <u>of</u> <u>spirit</u> (means troubling to the spirit, and as unfruitful as chasing after the wind).

Surely, concerning the works of nature and man, with all this being said. The imbalance between the things of God and the desires of the flesh reveals our wonderful Creator God is not satisfied with the nature of man.

Indeed, I believe the point the great preacher man is trying to make is clear, and he's saying that only God's works are fruitful, good, and pure, similar to the image of nature. But the works of men are weary and troubling to his spirit and as unfruitful as chasing after the wind.

It's easy to conclude that nature's works are more orderly than the works of man, and the great preacher man uses the sun, the wind, the rivers, and the sea to illustrate how orderly the works of God proceed, day after day.

However, the works of man are mostly unorderly and mostly done in vain, and they contrast with the natural order of things. This truth means the works of man are usually troubling to the spirit and are as fruitless as trying to catch the wind.

> **Ecclesiastes 1:15** (And the great preacher man says), that which is crooked cannot be made straight: and that which is <u>wanting</u> (means lacking, vanity, and the treasures of this world) cannot be numbered.

The great and wise preacher man stretched his brain to understand the order of things. The scriptures reveal the great preacher pondered many thoughts within his troubled heart, and all the mysteries of life puzzled him, and he wanted answers.

Furthermore, he told himself, lo, I am rich and wise and have many treasures and much wisdom. The great preacher said to himself, I have more knowledge than all the others who came before me and are living among me.

Yet, the great preacher man concluded, my spirit is troubled by the works of the flesh, and I am a man in the flesh chasing after the wind. The next curious scripture reveals the amount of thought the great preacher man put into everything under the sun.

Ecclesiastes 1:17 And I gave my heart to know wisdom, and to know madness and folly:

Ecclesiastes 1:17 I <u>perceived</u> (means he became aware of the fact) that <u>this</u> (wisdom, madness, and folly) is <u>vexation</u> <u>of</u> <u>spirit</u> (means troubling to the heart).

Ecclesiastes 1:18 For in much wisdom is much grief: And he that increaseth knowledge, increaseth sorrow.

The great preacher set his heart on things of beauty and used his money to build beautiful houses and plant beautiful vineyards. The great preacher made beautiful gardens and orchards, planted trees to bear fruit, and made many beautiful pools of water.

The great preacher man had servants, maidens, great possessions of cattle, many other animals, and much silver and gold. The great preacher had men singers, women singers, dancers, and various musical instruments, and whatever pleased him, he did.

It's easy to conclude that the great preacher man was extremely powerful, and he ruled over and judged many people, bought his manpower, and used his subjects to build beautiful projects. It's quite obvious; the great preacher man didn't have time to spare and didn't have much time for my Great God.

Ecclesiastes 2:10 And what so ever my eyes desired, I kept not from them, I withheld not my heart from any joy; For my heart rejoiced in all my labors: And <u>this</u> (pleasure of power and fulfillment) was my portion of all my labor.

The great preacher had wisdom and control and wielded the power of life and death over other men, and many people believe the preacher man was Solomon. But most likely, The Great Preacher Man is written literally, and the author was a great preacher, alias an assemblyman.

The great Preacher man sincerely admits all his accomplishments were meant to give him much pleasure. But in his golden years, his heart became keenly aware of the cycle of life. Sadly, his life would end lacking the greater knowledge, and he spent too much time misdirecting his energies.

The preacher man realized the things he worked all his life to build would outlast his life cycle. Indeed, his new-found awareness of the cycle of life means he was flesh and blood and created from the dirt of this Earth, and he has a short lifespan, the same as everyone else.

His newfound awareness reveals the pleasures he lived for were madness, folly, vanity, and troubling to his spirit. This conclusion means the great preacher man finally realized the truth, and after many years, he concluded his vanity lifestyle and his works weren't pleasing to God.

Furthermore, the great preacher man realized this reality of truth in his old age. His time to meet his Creator God and give account for himself was getting closer and closer every day. I am quite certain the great preacher man was concerned about whether or not his name is recorded in the Book of Life.

Positively, the great preacher found out it's troubling to the spirit if we labor for beautiful things and then be lazy at doing the works of God. I assure you the needed works of our great God are much more important than building beautiful structures and pools.

By observing creation and God's nature, the great preacher realized that the natural order of things coincides with His orderly design. As important as it is to build needed buildings and make improvements, it's equally as important to advance the gospel of God.

The great preacher man, including you and me, should heed nature and apply more order to our lives. This truth means we shouldn't toil in vain for too many beautiful things, let a great opportunity pass us by, and forget to lay up treasures in Heaven.

> **Ecclesiastes 2:11** Then <u>I</u> (the great preacher man) looked on all the works that my hands had <u>wrought</u> (means made), and on all the labor that I had labored to do: And, behold, all was <u>vanity</u> (means troubling to the spirit),

> **Ecclesiastes 2:11,** and there was <u>no</u> <u>profit</u> (means no real spiritual value to beautiful manmade things) under the sun.

The great preacher man was hard to satisfy, and he spent most of his life creating and building beautiful things. The great preacher realized he put too much emphasis on pleasuring himself, as most rich and powerful people do.

Although, in the end, he realized our purpose in life, it was after observing nature and the natural order of things. Surely, it's a wake-up call to reach our golden years and realize we haven't laid up treasures in Heaven.

Indeed, the great preacher assures us our purpose in life isn't to see how many beautiful things we can build or how much money we can accumulate. But our true purpose is to learn about the God of Heaven and Earth and apply our knowledge to evangelism.

Just imagine how much more rewarding it would've been to the great preacher if he had donated his years and set his heart on laying up treasures in Heaven. I believe the great preacher man influenced the people around him and could've guided many people to God.

I assure you his life would've been more rewarding if he had spent an equal amount of time and money doing evangelism for the Lord. Then, the works of his life wouldn't have been in vain because the works of the Lord cannot be considered vain.

I don't know how the great preacher was so rich, but he had everything of material value on this Earth a man could want. Still, with all his wisdom and money, he was searching for the meaning of life and the correct order of things, and he wasn't satisfied with how he spent the days of his life.

However, after the great preacher finally discovered the conclusion to the whole matter, he also discovered the meaning of life and the natural order of things. Whenever anyone discovers the conclusion to the whole matter, God will become more important to them than an abundance of materialism.

The *conclusion to the whole matter*, *the meaning of life*, and the natural order of things are the important things our God is trying to teach us. They are the only things on this Earth not considered vexation of the spirit and troubling to the soul.

Nor is the conclusion to the whole matter and the meaning of life as fruitless as chasing after the wind, and I am sure knowing the meaning of these two subjects will benefit our walk with God. However, resisting the natural order illustrates going in the wrong direction or stumbling around in the dark without a light.

Anyway, do not think the great preacher says we shouldn't work and labor for our keep and lay under a shade tree all day. Because work is good and extremely important to survival, we all need to labor for our bread and butter, and God says so.

However, I want you to know laboring for the riches of this world for the benefit of being rich fulfills the definition of vanity. Surely, too much importance on vanity could cause a person to be lukewarm or cold with our Great Savior God. The scriptures tell us the lukewarm and the cold do not have a home reserved for them in Heaven.

The great preacher earnestly sought to know the conclusion to the whole matter. After he realized godliness is better than folly and beautiful things, as light is much better than darkness, His heart changed, and he wanted a closer relationship with God.

I assure you the conclusion to the whole matter and the meaning of life magnifies the importance of separating vanity from godliness. I am certain vanity and godliness aren't a compatible combination. Furthermore, I am sure Satan has ruined many good men by showing them the path to gain riches.

The great preacher used himself and nature as examples to explain the important order of things. This revelation means the preacher realized wise men walk in the perfect ways of God and fools desire too much vanity. Indeed, if the Lord were to ask you what good will it do to gain the whole world if you lose your soul chasing riches, what would you say, rich man?

After being misguided for many years, the great preacher man concluded that the wise man and the fool would conform to the order of things someday and face the same fate, called death. Truly, as we live daily, you and I would be wise to learn a lesson from the great preacher and live by the conclusion to the whole matter.

Therefore, if a person has wisdom, the thought of death and the hereafter and where they'll spend eternity should be the uttermost important thing on their mind, rather than wanting to be more powerful and richer than other men. Sadly, vanity is the reason many men and women will not think about the rules of God and burn in Hell because they love riches the most.

The great preacher man concluded wanting to build more beautiful things than we need takes away our time with God. The great preacher realized the works of the flesh were soon forgotten, and a wise man will say he mostly wasted his life away chasing vanity.

Furthermore, another person coming after us will spend our excessive gain, regardless of whether we are foolish or wise. However, after the death of our flesh, it'll be too late to change our autobiography of life or erase anything written in the Book of Life.

Therefore, ungodly men and women having too much excess will look foolish in their own eyes on Judgment Day. However, on Judgement Day, we cannot trade ungodliness for godliness from the pits of Hell, even after realizing the natural order of things.

Therefore, righteousness, conversion, and the natural order of things must be found while still alive, mainly because conversion to a Christ-like character doesn't happen from the realms of Hell, and too late is too late to learn the natural order of things.

Therefore, let's take our example from nature and submit ourselves to the natural order, and to save your soul, always remember the conclusion to the whole matter is to reverence God and keep His commandments, which is man's whole duty.

I assure you the important structure of reality is to lay up treasures in Heaven, walk in the ways of God, and secure immortality. Everything else is vexation and vanity and troubling to our spirit. Truly, the natural order of things parallels God's perfect word, and loving the God of creation and his word should be as natural as drinking water.

CHAPTER THIRTY-TWO

THE SECOND PASSOVER

This need-to-know story is about the Second Passover, and because we are thankful to Yeshua for His sacrifice, you and I should call it by the correct name instead of a pagan name. Even though the corridors of time prove, most professing Christians have called it by the wrong name.

I assure you, there's no logical reason, nor is there a good excuse for calling the Second Passover by the wrong name, especially when calling it by the right name is so easy. I know calling it by the right name will please God because His Son was the sacrifice on the cross, and His Father wants us to illustrate our respect to Him.

Furthermore, the Father, the Son, and the Holy Ghost would appreciate us calling the resurrection event by the correct name. Truly, the great Second Passover shouldn't be hard to understand, and it's easy to apply the correct name to the resurrection of Yeshua.

The blood-drenched Second Passover is the greatest memorial event in the history of Christianity, and it brings into remembrance the death, burial, and resurrection of the Son of God. I guarantee, no other acts of compassion equal the sacrifice of Yeshua.

I assure you that our great ruling God from above expects respect from us, and he tells us to remember and keep the Passover of the Lamb. Mainly because the meaningful sacrificial Passover is for every generation a memorial, and it should be remembered by Christians forever.

The first eventful Passover, consisting of a literal lamb, an animal among the flock in the pasture, points to the supernatural deliverance of His people, who were delivered from a life of bondage to the cruel Egyptian people and from the wicked Lucifer.

I declare that the Second Passover is more serious than the First Passover because it symbolizes the blood of Jesus Christ and is a greater memorial than the First Passover memorial. I assure you the blood of a literal lamb cannot compare to the blood of the Lamb of God.

The two meaningful Passovers are holy events and deserve the correctness of the identification. I want you to know it's blasphemous and disrespectful for a Christian to call the first and second Passover by the pagan name of Easter.

I purposely write my stories about the Father, the Son, and the Holy Ghost with much passion, and I am a man in love with the revealing word of God. When incorrectness comes to my attention, I try to expose whatever it is and teach the truth.

Although, I think many professing Christians aren't paying enough attention to the perfect word of God, and not paying enough attention means correctness will elude them to some degree. Sadly, it's during times like this that incorrectness gets a foothold it shouldn't have in Christianity.

Indeed, it makes me sad to speak so bluntly concerning passive Christians coasting through Christianity, and coasting through Christianity is similar to a car running out of gas and slowly rolling to a stop. Truly, I assure you, coasting through Christianity is much more serious than a car running out of gas.

Therefore, the main reason I speak so bluntly about the things of God is that I passionately love correctness and authenticity. I believe blunt and straight talk is the arrow of truth; hopefully, the truth is the only sword sharp enough to pierce thick skulls.

I assure you, irreverent and disrespectful things in the churches must be exposed, and for the glory of God, disrespectful things need to be pierced through the heart and cut asunder. For the benefit of preserving authenticity, the sword of the Lord does the best cutting.

Undoubtedly, many Sun-day Christians must wonder why they don't see more miracles happen in their church. I am certain it's hard for them to understand why; they do not see more healing and prayers answered in the house of God.

One reason may be that too many sacrilegious and disrespectful things are present in the house of God. I severely warn you irreverent and disrespectful things anger our God, and anger doesn't promote favor from above or gain any divine blessings.

Christians can chant and sing about what it's like up there and put themselves in an emotional state of mind. But until they submit themselves to the whole truth and abort sacrilegious and disrespectful practices within the house of God.

Then, they may be unable to claim God's promises and blessings regardless of whether they know what they are doing. But at the very least, there are two important things professing Sun-day Christians can do to improve their standing with God.

The first one is to quit keeping the Sun Day Sabbath Day and start keeping the holy, sacred, and seventh day Sabbath Day. The second thing professing Christians must do to improve themselves with God is to start calling the death, burial, and resurrection of Jesus Christ by the sacred name of *Passover*.

Indeed, do not call the death, burial, and resurrection of the wonderful Son of God by the ungodly pagan name of Easter. If we call His resurrection from death Easter, it illustrates a lack of understanding and reveals an understudied Christian.

The first Passover is a perfect example of love shown to a suppressed people who lived in bondage to the Egyptians and Lucifer for four hundred and thirty years. In both cases, it was our Supernatural God and the blood of the Lamb, able to deliver souls from slavery and the wrath of the death angel.

Therefore, glory, honor, and love belong to Israel's wonderful God and the Son of God, alias the Lamb, sacrificed on the wooden cross. I am certain the human race wouldn't be here today if it weren't for them.

Indeed, remembrance of the First Passover and the Second Passover is seriously important and more special than any other event for Christians to remember forever. I want you to know calling it by the right name illustrates a caring, Bible-savvy Christian.

The wonderful Second Passover is an unequaled memorial, which we observe to express great appreciation and unforgotten love. Surely, all the love the God of Heaven and Earth and His Son have expressed toward us, we need to express it back to them and adhere to His authenticity.

Bible scriptures reveal that the wonderful Second Passover event was written about many years ago. It was prophesied in the book of Isaiah, chapter fifty-three, that our wonderful Son of God will suffer death at the hands of His enemies and the enemies of Christianity.

Furthermore, the Bible tells me He arose from the grave on the third day. Not to say, He laid in the grave three days because He didn't. By the way, the third day was most likely at the end of the seventh day, Sabbath Day, and not on Sun Day.

Simply because from Wednesday evening at three o'clock until Saturday evening at three o'clock is three days. Surely, it's perfect for Christ to rise at the end of the established rest day. Since it's a special day, proclaimed and set in motion from the first Earth age.

This truth means from the beginning of creation, the seventh day rest day was established by the unchangeable word of God. And it's fitting to believe the faithful Son of God arose from His rest place at the end of the established rest day.

Conclusively, after the Son of God's death, burial, and resurrection, we who believe in Him as our Savior are granted a special privilege. The special privilege allows us to repent and change whenever we make a mistake and are regretful for doing wrong.

Therefore, it's fitting and correct to say repentance and remission of sin should be preached in His name among all nations, beginning at Jerusalem. Truly, within this next enlightenment scripture, the wise Apostle Paul tells us Jesus is our Passover.

Indeed, I am certain the beautiful Son of God is why the death angel passes over us. Surely, calling His death on the cross event by the identification name of a fertility goddess and her ritual illustrates an uncompassionate thing to do to the Savior who died for all humankind.

The Second Passover, written in the next teaching scripture, confirms the death, burial, and resurrection. Indeed, if the Bible confirms the truth, we should call it the Second Passover, and there's no reason we should call it by another name than what Paul teaches.

1 Corinthians 5:7 (The Apostle Paul says), forever Christ our Passover is sacrificed for us.

The word forever means what it says, and the word Passover cannot correctly be exchanged for any other word, such as Easter. Sadly, when we call the Passover by the name of Easter, then we are calling the Passover an ungodly name, paralleling an ungodly event.

Forever, after the wonderful Son of God died on the cross, He became our Passover sacrifice for sin. Adding bunny rabbits and eggs and a fertility goddess celebration day to His death event illustrates an ungodly thing to do to our Savior from the fires of Hell.

Indeed, for the benefit of higher learning, greater understanding, correct definition, and godliness. Please be Bible-savvy and recognize it's irreverent, disrespectful, and ungodly to call the Passover sacrifice of Jesus Christ by the pagan name of Easter.

Furthermore, Yeshua's death, burial, and resurrection are memorialized by the feast of Passover. The word Easter should be ugly and forgotten, especially by all professing Christians who love correctness. I must tell you some study time in the gospel of God lessens the chance of making mistakes.

The next two informative scriptures will thoroughly explain the importance and the ability of the blood of Christ. I assure you the precious blood of Christ hasn't any connection to bunny rabbits, a fertility goddess, or any pagan practice. Truly, if I were you, I wouldn't practice the traditions of men or connect them to Yeshua's death, burial, and resurrection.

1 Peter 1:18 For as much as ye know that ye were not <u>redeemed</u> (means not cleansed, or saved) with <u>corruptible</u> <u>things</u>, as silver and gold, from your <u>vain</u> <u>conversation</u> (means foolish ways) by the traditions of your fathers.

1 Peter 1:19 But with the precious blood of Christ**,** as of a lamb without <u>blemish</u> (means without fault) and without <u>spot</u> (means without sin).

1 Peter 1:20, who <u>verily</u> (means truly) was <u>foreordained</u> (means established and chosen) before the foundation of the world, but was <u>manifest</u> (means revealed) in these last times for you.

Indeed, our incorruptible Passover Lamb, who holds back the hand of the death angel, is the wonderful Son of God. Please realize our redemption and deliverance from sin came at the price of His blood, which Yeshua voluntarily gave to cleanse us of sin.

Surely, it should be duly noted, and we should realize something extremely important about the wonderful Savior God. The same hand restraining the death angel can also release the hand of the death angel, and this life in the flesh is a serious life-and-death test.

I want you to know that God's compassionate and wonderful Son is a picture of pure and undefiled love. The proof is that He willingly sacrificed His life and suffered a horrible death to redeem us from the bondage of sin and save us from the fires of Hell.

Indeed, there's no greater love than the sincere love Jesus illustrated upon the cross for all sinners living on this Earth. The blood sacrifice He made approximately two thousand years ago is for every generation determined to believe in Him.

Therefore, everyone, regardless of race, gender, or color, who sincerely believes in Him is a member of God's living church. Indeed, every member of the living church of God glorifies the Father and His Son from wherever they stand on this Earth.

There's another memorial, personal and special, besides the memorial of Yeshua's death, burial, and resurrection. This special memorial I am speaking about isn't the first Passover during the second Earth age known to happen in Egypt at the time of Moses.

The special and personal memorial I am talking about concerns all believers in Christ, and it's a thankful emotion dedicated to Yeshua and the memorial planted inside our hearts. The special memorial planted inside our hearts causes us to be thankful to the beautiful Son of God every moment we live and breathe.

I assure you the Father, the Son of God, and the word of God are memorialized by our hearts' love for them. However, the Second Passover memorializes the death, burial, and resurrection of Yeshua, the compassionate Son of God.

The sacrificing Second Passover was paid for with the blood of Christ, and He was a gentle Lamb who walked among the wolves, snakes, and vipers in Jerusalem. Sadly, He suffered much physical abuse and cruel humiliation at the hands of the Roman soldiers.

His painful ordeal includes suffering and humiliation at the hands of Herod the Second, Pilate, the chief priests, and the scribes. I am certain He allowed this cruelty to happen to Him because He loves you and me and wants us to be His children in His kingdom.

I want you to know the Second Passover is more significant than the First Passover, and it's because the blood of a literal lamb cannot compare to the blood of the Son of God. Truly, the promise saying we can rise at the first resurrection is made possible because of His blood sacrifice.

Therefore, the memorial of Jesus Christ shouldn't in any way be identified by the pagan name, Easter, and well-studied Christians know the truth and do not call the special Second Passover by the pagan name of Easter.

However, the passive, the less caring, and the understudied Christians do not know that Yeshua's death, burial, and resurrection are called the Second Passover. It's a shame this ongoing compromise hasn't been challenged or changed in the last two thousand years.

Conclusively, if you do not know the correct name of Yeshua's death, burial, and resurrection, then your lack of bible knowledge proves you need to study the revealing word of God much more than you do.

Mainly to show yourself concerned about knowing the truth, and the truth is gained by knowing the wonderful word of God. But sadly, to say, there's a famine in this land for the meat of Christianity, and the meat is the meal more Christians need to eat.

CHAPTER THIRTY-THREE

PRIVILEGED OR NOT

This sad story, concerning the fate of all the unbelievers, called *Privileged Or Not,* portrays ungodly men and women who rejected the required word of God and died and went to Hell. It's easy to conclude that Hell's residents aren't privileged people, and they know it and hate God.

However, the mark of the beast's residents of Hell is prophesized to come back upon this Earth again after the gates of Hell are opened. But I want you to know they'll not have flesh and blood bodies when they return. **Revelation 9:2** reveals an angel opening the bottomless pit, and they'll parallel having an indestructible body as before the great flood.

This look into the future story also portrays ungodly men and women still alive on the surface of this Earth when the gates of Hell are opened. Indeed, when the inhabitants of Hell ascend upon this Earth, they'll mix bloodlines again, and it'll be with whoever has the mark of the beast.

Believing that everything coming out of Hell will have the mark of the beast makes sense, and the bloodline mixing, when they come out of Hell, will be the mark of the beast from Hell, mixing with the mark of the beast people still alive on the Earth.

During the great last days of tribulation, three different bloodlines will be back on this Earth again simultaneously. The three old bloodlines will be here simultaneously, as before the great cleansing flood, during the wicked first Earth age.

Most likely, the cursed and ungodly men and women who failed to find our Great Savior God still alive in the flesh. They'll become victims of the Mark of the Beast clique and the protection seal of God they'll not receive.

During the great tribulation time, the flesh and blood people living on this Earth with the mark of the beast might even believe Satan will defeat God, and they'll be elite people. They'll probably believe they'll be privileged characters, worship Lucifer, and live on this Earth forever.

Indeed, because of their liberal compatibility with whoever ascends out of Hell and because they reject our Great Creator God as their Savior God, it will seem that the evil residents from Hell will own this Earth for eternity.

However, suppose ungodly sinners, who have the mark of the beast, consider their compatibility as an asset or a comrade link to Lucifer. In that case, they think they'll be treated like the elite during the great and mysterious tribulation time when the children of God are being persecuted.

Then I want you to know their wild imagination has overcome their perception of reality, and blindness of the mind is hiding the truth from them because the mark of the beast will cause the unbelievers trouble from the rebellious angels and God.

Positively, I want you to know that God's wrath and anger is the tribulation time for whoever is ungodly. I am certain whoever has the mark of the beast will be troubled by my Great God and the demons from Hell who want them transformed into fighting machines.

The wicked Lucifer wants an army of fighting machines and will not be loyal to any man or woman, and being ungodly and having the mark of the beast will not help anyone's plight during the great tribulation time. I assure you, the mark of the beast will not be an asset to anyone after the tares are separated from the wheat and burned like the chaff on the threshing floor.

This truth means if you have the mark of the beast, the supernatural plagues sent by the all-mighty God of creation are your plagues. Maybe, after a while, plagued ungodly men will realize the mark of the beast is more hurtful to them than helpful.

Furthermore, the wicked and rebellious Lucifer will not be able to relieve the mark of the beast people from the suffering of the plagues God pours on them from the Heavens above. I am certain that the only thing that'll bother Lucifer will be his knowledge, knowing that the warrior Son of God is coming after him.

Indeed, ungodly men would rather die than suffer from boils and sores not designed to kill them because the boils and the sores will cause them unbearable torment and pain. But not death, even though the mark of the beast people might prefer death.

Suppose any specific events can cause the memory of an ungodly person's life to flash before their eyes. I am sure it'll be the terrible tribulation time, the mark of the beast, and the knowledge of eternal salvation is lost, especially since they know they could've had a Savior and lived forever.

I am certain that lost men and women will recall their lifestyle, especially after they know the special privilege they've lost and why they'll not be invited to live in the wonderful kingdom of God.

Beyond the shadow of a doubt, lost men and women will think about their rebellious lifestyle and how life could've turned out better for them. I believe they'll regret their constant rejection of our Supreme God and every sin they've ever committed.

I am certain most people will think about their illogical servitude to ungodliness, and maybe they'll wonder why they illogically abhorred our Great Creator God's perfect and required word. Even though hindsight isn't worth much, the scales will fall from their eyes, and they'll know they should've loved my creator God.

Surely, after living all their life in rejection of God's wonderful word, they've accepted the horrible mark of the beast and fallen prey to the supernatural plagues of boils and sores, as prophesized in the great book of Revelation.

Then they'll know they've served the wrong god and lived the wrong lifestyle. I want you to know if we die cold or lukewarm toward God, then we'll have the mark of the beast during the tribulation time, too. My heart is sad because some men and women will not secure salvation, and the foresight, I will tell you, is to love God and be hot and on fire for His gospel.

Indeed, Lucifer is the wicked god of rebellion, and wrath is designated for him and his followers, and the final judgment will catch up to all of them. Whether we realize it or not, we are being weighed in balance scales as we live and breathe daily.

However, as for now, the important things in this life, such as securing eternal salvation, seem to elude most people because most people would rather not think about tomorrow and not think about life after death.

However, as we live and breathe and make our way through life on this unstable Earth before the death of our flesh. Be assured that life after death cannot be changed after we die, and the gift of grace isn't available to the lost and those who are dead.

This truth means you should know for certain before you die that the mark of the beast is irreversible, and it cannot be changed back once it's taken. I want you to realize being hot and on fire for the word of God is our only mark of the beast repellant.

I am certain the terrible things prophesized to happen to the unbelievers during the great tribulation time. It'll cause many ungodly men and women who have the mark of the beast to wish they could do it again and live for the glory of God.

During the great tribulation time, I believe many ungodly and hardhearted men and women will live on this Earth, and I am certain all of them will wish they had the name of God written on their forehead. Since the name of God written on them is the only mark that protects them from the reaper angels and the Son of God, who will also be a reaper with a sickle in His hand.

Indeed, having the condemning numbers six, six, and six representing the mark of the beast and their loyalty to Lucifer, the wicked Lucifer will have a great army to rise from the pits of Hell, and all of them will have his mark and be reaped from the Earth.

Furthermore, suppose the abomination of desolation could have things his way during the great tribulation time. In that case, Lucifer would finish his unfinished work; he started during the first Earth age, before the great cleansing flood.

Then again, for the second time, he and the other rebellious angels would subdue this Earth, and everyone would worship them. They would try to kill off the male population and use the females to start a mixed bloodline again for the second time.

Lucifer would create his new Heaven upon this Earth, consisting of only rebellious angelic creations and mixed bloodline creations. Again, the evil Lucifer would have his children of a mixed bloodline, and it would be again, as he ruled on this Earth four thousand years ago before the great flood.

They would have the heritage of his bloodline, like the bloodline of Cain, and Cain was his first mixed bloodline son. Furthermore, if you wonder where Cain is today, consider the ungodly's residence, and you'll find the murderer, Cain, living among them in Hell.

I assure you, it's a fitting description of Lucifer when he's called by his alias name, the abomination of desolation, mainly because Lucifer has a plan and desires to eradicate mankind from total existence through death or bloodline transformation.

However, there's a Highest God in Heaven, and He's not going to let Lucifer have his way with mankind, and He's the enemy of Lucifer. He will save a remnant of mankind who love Him and His righteousness, as stipulated by His perfect commandments.

His remnant of loyal believers will be the humble and peaceful people; He's purposely chosen to keep them alive during the wonderful and special thousand-year millennium. I pray because you love God; I hope you'll be included in the peaceful millennium.

However, before the thousand-year millennium starts, the wicked Lucifer will be turned loose on this Earth and will be in his physical form. This truth means the opening of the bottomless pit and the terrible tribulation time before Christ's second return is beginning.

These events start the abomination of desolation and countdown to destruction and eternal damnation. I want you to know that Lucifer's countdown comes before the prophesized millennium begins, and Lucifer will spend this time readying himself to battle with the Son of God.

Even though the abomination of desolation is the dominant figure on the Earth, during the terrible tribulation time, our Most High God will trouble him and persecute his environment with the vials of the seven plagues.

Furthermore, I assure you, the great tribulation time is for compensation, designed specifically against ungodly people. Truly, the conclusion reveals ungodly people marked by the beast will not be privileged by the evil abomination of desolation.

However, they will be the victims of judgment and suffer recompense from the Heavens above. After the released residents of Hell kill ungodly men and women, they'll descend into Hell, and their spirits will be redesigned into fierce fighting creatures.

Conclusively, regardless of the generation, whoever descended into Hell is wearing the beast's mark, and so is everyone coming out of the pits of Hell after an angel from Heaven opens the gates. The whole Earth will look like a floodgate opened, flooding this Earth with the mark of the beast gang.

Indeed, the residents leaving Hell will wear the mark of the beast when they come out of Hell. Two different types of people will fight the great battle for planet Earth at the end of the tribulation time. One type will be godly, and the other type will be ungodly.

I am certain the Son of God will battle the abomination of desolation, alias Lucifer. I believe whoever has the seal of God on their forehead will be battling whoever has the mark of the beast.

Positively, now is your important moment to choose, so pick the side of the fence you want to be on as soon as possible and be loyal to one or the other master you want to serve because there are no in-between choices. At the end of the tribulation battle, our final destiny will coincide with the mark of the beast or the seal of God.

CHAPTER THIRTY-FOUR

THORNS

This revealing story, *Thorns*, is a metaphor story filled with the truth, and it's not talking about the sharp wooden thorns growing on a tree that pierce and puncture our skin and physically hurt us. I want you to realize the literal thorn tree isn't a part of this story, but you will realize we have thorns.

The definition of thorns in this metaphor story symbolizes the tares and the chaff, the male goats, and all the unbelievers; God separates from the sheep. The sheep are His people who believe in Him, and in their next life, they will be nobles, saints, and members of royalty.

However, in this metaphor story, the thorns are identified as ungodly men and women, and whoever troubles this world rejects the righteous ways designed by God's perfect and infallible word. I assure you that in their next life, the thorns will not be nobles, saints, and members of royalty.

This revealing story, designed to divide two types of people, illustrates the characteristic differences between the thorns and fruitful works and the kind of people leaning to the left and right. Sadly, the thorns are indifferent people and support ungodliness, and the believers in God are passionate and support godliness.

The vicious thorns are also the bad seed planted on this Earth by the wicked Lucifer and the other rebellious angels, and since the beginning of mankind, the thorns have been God's number one enemy and our enemy. Sadly, many of the thorns are invisible and hide their image and must expose themselves before we can identify them.

The main purpose of the thorns is to choke out and destroy the word of God, or at the least, keep it from growing strong. Sadly, the thorns are more than demon angels and this society of people we live in has many *liberal thorns*, and they are restricting the wheat from growing properly.

I assure you many of the wicked thorns in this world are extremely rich, powerful, and ungodly. Indeed, if they serve Lucifer well, then the powerful Lucifer will bless his thorns with an abundance of prosperity, and he will bless them with authority to rule over many men and women.

Therefore, if you are under the impression the wicked Lucifer doesn't use prosperity to pull men away from the God of Heaven and Earth, then you are wrong mainly because Lucifer uses the riches of this world to recruit many of his servants of darkness.

Furthermore, I am certain the wicked Lucifer doesn't use the poor people on this Earth nearly as much as he uses the rich. But still, the wicked Lucifer recruits poor people, too. Sadly, a lack of Bible knowledge and love for the gospel of God is the formula for a recruit into the army of Satan.

However, concerning you, me, and everyone else, it's better for the poor man who happily walks with integrity and kindness rather than the rich man, who walks in arrogance, pride, and heart-hardness. Sadly, when the heart will not soften and walk in the ways of God, we are probably looking at a thorn.

It's for certain: if you want to be rich, you should be extremely careful about how you obtain your riches. Truly, if you succeed at getting rich, be careful, and do not let the ill-gotten riches of this world turn you into a hardhearted thorn.

The next declaration scripture entwines rich men, unfruitful works, and the thorns together. For this important reason, take heed, rich man, and not be the person who heareth the word of God among the thorns, listens for a moment and forgets the godliness God's word represents.

Matthew 13:22 He also that receiveth <u>seed</u> (means heareth the word of God) among the <u>thorns</u>, (means people attached to this material world) is he that heareth the word. The cares of this world and the deceitfulness of riches choke the word, and he becomes unfruitful (which means he becomes bare, useless, without righteous or godly works).

Often, when casually interested people, not known to hunger for His wonderful word, hear God's word somewhere in the world, and like it, they are given a chance to repent and be saved. In the beginning, they love it, at least until the word of God interferes with their ambition for wealth and prosperity and the ungodly functions in this world.

They are the people snagged by the thorns attached to this material world, and they keep looking back the same way Lot's wife looked back. They are the undecided people who purposely put the cares of this world first and the required word of God last.

Conclusively, in this unstable and diverse generation, it appears correct to say most people put material gain and the pleasures of this world first. This statement means the thorns have nearly choked out the needed word of God, and casually interested people will rarely be hot and on fire for His gospel.

Mainly because the excellent word of God doesn't seem to be liked much by the majority of this world, and it's too conservative for most people. However, immorality and greed, same-sex marriage, the love of money, and *liberalism* all seem to be accepted more by the world than the lifesaving word of God, created to set men free from sin.

Indeed, when the righteous word of God becomes tangled and hindered by the thorns and receives the silent treatment. It becomes unfruitful and lost, and it's not of any help to the lukewarm and cold person in this world. Who cannot conform to the temperature of hot, required by the rules of God? Sadly, the lukewarm and cold thorns are usually the reason why the temperature does not rise inside our hearts.

The temperature of hot and the required rules of God are His excellent Ten Commandments, and they bother people, tangled in the thorns. Indeed, because of ungodly characteristics, thorns are compatible with the cold and the lukewarm person.

Even though the required word of God provides the only hope and instructions designed to win the prize of immortality, most people in this world appear to be blind and deaf to a large degree. Sadly, because of spiritual blindness, they fail to understand the benefits of the gospel of God.

The perfect word of God says the deceitfulness of riches will choke out the wonderful word of God, especially whenever men and women make wealth their master. It's easy to conclude this is an out-of-control, money-hungry world, so the love of money is the root of all evil.

In our wild, mixed-up world today, I want you to know that only a few men and women seem to remember an intangible fact beneficial to the gift of salvation. The wonderful Most High Creator God, the loyal counsel in Heaven, the loyal, holy ones, and the angels can see everything we do and hear every word we say, and it's recorded in the Book of Life.

Still, most of us are unaware; we are being watched and heard by the saints who went on before us in Heaven. Undoubtedly, in their eyes, we limited-time humans must appear to be a sad lot of people, easily persuaded by the lure of material gain and the pleasures of sin.

Indeed, sadly, we appear to be weak-minded people who put too much emphasis on wealth and prosperity during the short time we live on this Earth. Money lovers never seem to realize the whole duty of man is to love God and live by His righteous ways.

It appears true that the nature of men and women is mostly corrupt, wicked, deceitful, and not strong in the excellent word of God. It also appears true that most of us desire wealth and all the pleasures we can obtain more than we desire God's knowledge.

Indeed, it's how we are until we are old and feeble—and maybe, living on our death bed and afraid of dying lost. This truth means that all men and women will remember God during our last days of life but will not know where they stand with God until Judgment time.

Mainly because they do not know or understand the word of God, and it's because they rejected it for most of their life. Truly, we can probably say and conclude the thorns choked out the needed word of God before they could grasp and respect it.

Indeed, all people need to study and understand the excellent and wonderful King James Bible. It consists of approximately seven hundred and eighty thousand important words, and their significance is off the chart of importance, and falling in love with it will increase our godliness.

However, the extremely important Judgment Scales of God consists of only three important words. I want you to realize these three important words include everything we need to understand about our coming judgment, and what I am telling you is summed up in the conclusion of truth.

Therefore, always remember the extreme importance of these three accurate Judgment Scale words, especially since we all identify with one of them. The Bible assures all of us are judged by the three indicator words: hot, cold, and lukewarm.

Conclusively, when the thorns choke out the needed word of God, they leave behind the cold and the lukewarm. Sadly, the thorns might think God will forget about the Judgment words, and they forget about Him until the last moment, until the truth emerges from behind an uncaring mind. Sadly, fear grips and shakes their souls, and like other passive and indifferent people in this world, they depend on last-minute deathbed salvation.

I am unsure; anyone can get on fire for God's wonderful word while lying on their deathbed, and most likely, they cannot, but the wonderful gift of mercy belongs to our Great God, who gets the last say. However, I must tell you receiving mercy on the deathbed is a gamble not worth taking.

I am certain deathbed salvation isn't an established lifestyle, and it cannot prove our sincere love for God. But deathbed salvation does prove we've spent our entire lifetime not willing to convert to Christianity and be fully committed to His righteous word.

Indeed, I believe some diversions can create a thorn; the love of money is one of those diversions. Without a doubt, I can correctly say that too much love for money is one characteristic illustrating the ability to reduce our love for our God, and we cannot serve both.

Sometimes, the love of money is the reason for a terrible fever, which can consume and redirect our focus from God to the cares of this world. Until we are no longer rooted in good ground and are numb to the expectations of God and on the deathbed, we will be gambling on the gift of mercy.

This truth means the love of riches and spending all our time chasing after money illustrates us neglecting God and being caught in a terrible thorn trap. Sadly, I must tell you, the thorns can choke out the word of God, and too many thorns will erase the grand prize of immortality.

Indeed, the thorns in this story have a symbolic definition, and they can hurt us much more than the piercing of the flesh. I believe most of us have more than one thorn in our side, similar to how the changed for the better Apostle Paul had a thorn in his side.

I am certain another word, among many words included in the definition of thorns, is sin. I want you to realize for the benefit of reducing hurt, every rebellious act attached to sin adds another thorn in our side. For the well-being of our souls, I must tell you, compromising God's word is the worst thing we can do, but living by His commandments is the best thing we can do.

Sin hurts our hearts, pierces our conscience, and grieves our memory, even after the blood of the Lamb saves us and gives us a new life. I am sure a thorn collector lives a troubled life, and too many thorns equal an ungodly lifestyle. For this reason, I advise you not to live ungodly and be a thorn collector.

Indeed, the wrong things we've done in our past are a thorn in our hearts, and none of us have a perfect past. Without hesitation, I dare say every man and woman alive has a thorn piercing their heart, and I am sure all men and women wish they didn't have thorns piercing their hearts.

However, as the loyal and humbled Apostle, Paul had to live with a hurting thorn in his side, so will you and I have to live with a thorn hurting our hearts. But at least regretting thorns illuminates a changed heart and a newfound hate for Satan and sin.

Beyond the shadow of a doubt, thorns, alias sins, cause regret and shame but can increase our desire to do better. This realization means we cannot undo our past regardless of what we've done, but we can repent, change, and live a better life each day.

Indeed, I want you to know that conversion to Christianity will not remove the thorns embedded inside our conscience. Nor will conversion to

Christianity erase our previous mistakes or reduce the damage we've done in our sinful past.

However, I am certain that sincere conversion to Christianity can stop us from multiplying many more thorns, and I am convinced the new person in Christ tries hard to avoid the thorn tree. I want you to know the word of God doesn't have thorns, and we can sleep soundly on a pillow stitched together with His gospel truth.

Indeed, hurting thorns grow from compromises, making us feel shame and bothering our conscience, such as adultery, fornication, divorce, a lack of loyalty, murder, and deceptions of all sorts. Undoubtedly, every one of these mentioned compromises adds thorns to our hearts.

Conclusively, repentance and change will absolve us of these sinful things. But we all know through personal experience repentance and change don't take away the painful thorns in our hearts. However, knowing we changed into better people eases the pain caused by the thorns.

I assure you, and you do need to know the wicked and rebellious Satan is a powerful enemy, and all the thorn bushes belong to him. He purposely plants them abundantly within the pathway of every man, woman, and child, and calling him a thorn tree is appropriate.

This truth means his rebellious ways can put thorns in our hearts, and the righteous ways of God can shield us from his thorns. However, we need to avoid as many thorn bushes as possible, and the Ten Commandments are our map leading us around the thorn bushes.

Therefore, I urgently tell you we need to utilize the righteous Ten Commandments of God every day of our lives. We must trust them completely and be glad they expose the thorns. Sadly, I conclude that life is a road laden with thorns, and as we journey to the end of the road, we've all been punctured in our hearts by a thorn or two.

Indeed, the next scripture reveals that if we say we do not sin, we lie, which means that as hard as we try, we cannot be perfect. But if we walk in the light and have fellowship one with another, then the blood of Yeshua will cleaneth us from all sin.

> **1 John:8** If we say that we have no sin, we deceive ourselves, and the truth is not in us.

> **1 John:9** If we confess our sins, He is faithful, forgiving us, and cleanses us from all unrighteousness.

> **1 John:10** If we say that we have not sinned, we make Him a liar, and His word is not in us.

Before this story ends, I want you to know that the wonderful Son of God allowed Himself to be nailed to the cross so that we can repent and change. Truly, since we cannot escape the piercing of the thorns, we can repent, change, and be forgiven.

CHAPTER THIRTY-FIVE

SELF-MADE BLESSINGS OR DIVINE BLESSINGS

Without a doubt, many of us wonder where our blessings come from or the reason for our blessings, and it's a good question; we can't always answer correctly. This truth about people's ideas means that not all blessings come from God, nor does He pick and choose everyone blessed with health and wealth.

Simply because many dreams are self-made by men and women, who labor through the works of their hands and the works of their brains, and most of the time, prosperity is a reward for working hard, and we see the results of hard-working people, illustrated by the material things they gain.

However, I want you to realize working hard to gain prosperity cannot always be considered a divine blessing from our wonderful God. Even though many believe prosperity is a one-hundred percent blessing from God, it's wishful thinking to believe God is the reason for every rich man.

I assure you that a sign of prosperity isn't necessarily a divine blessing from God but could result from perseverance and steadfast labor. Neither are all hardships a curse, nor is a disadvantage in life a divine punishment from God.

Many hardships can result from laziness, bad luck, poor education, and bad health could result from eating and living the wrong lifestyle. Too many times, people associate great prosperity and good health with blessings from the God of Heaven and Earth.

I am certain it's an assumption to believe the God of Heaven and Earth controls every aspect of our prosperity, hardships, and health. Surely, to believe otherwise would be to believe we haven't any free will and are His puppets on a string.

Therefore, it's hard to determine the identity of a blessing from God and a self-made blessing from toils and labor. In most circumstances, not many people realize the source of their blessings, and it's because of a lack of Bible knowledge and a big imagination.

Truly, most people cannot say for certain whether their blessings, curses, and hardships are self-made or a divine call from God. This truth means, most of the time, we do not know whether we are in total control of our lives or if an outside force is directing our footsteps.

Indeed, believers and unbelievers must consider if an invisible force controls us and whether or not the outside force compels us to do many things we do. Truly, because we know we aren't alone in this world, we would be wise to realize that the air's spirits will try to influence us.

Furthermore, we must realize we have a part to play in this game of life and death. Unless spiritual blindness hinders our perception, we must understand that we are responsible for our decisions, regardless of spiritual influence, simply because we can reject demonic guidance and accept the Holy Ghost's influence.

I am certain there are different types of invisible supernatural forces among us. Through the power of telepathy, they can influence our behavior and our emotions to some unknown degree. For this reason, we must scrutinize our every decision and make sure we aren't going against the will of God.

Indeed, there's also a fighting free will within us, influenced by the strength of our hearts and the beautiful Holy Ghost. Remember, there's one thing for certain, and it's something we all probably realize about ourselves without being told by anyone.

We have to fight against our sinful nature and fight against the invisible demonic evil spirits of the air. However, if we aren't a warrior for the wonderful word of God, then our sinful nature will drift more and more out of control.

Positively, the wicked Lucifer, alias the terrible devil, is an invisible demonic spirit, and his evil spirit compels men and women to be godless, unclean, and against Christ. Truly, because he hates our Great Creator God, he directs his hate toward everyone who loves God.

We must use our free will to fight against the compulsion to be disobedient to God's laws and life-saving commandments. I hope you realize this is our responsibility; we are responsible for doing it for ourselves. We cannot journey through this world without battling opposition, and regardless of the circumstance, God expects us to fight the temptation to sin.

Our Great Most High God can reward men and women with divine blessings because they try their best to do His will, and the formula for riding upon the high places of this Earth is achieved because we do His will. Indeed, when our lifestyle aligns with His will, we are a candidate to receive divine blessings.

Furthermore, I do not believe in my heart; the God of Heaven and Earth will stand idly by, watch, and do nothing to help His faithful people in distress. But He gives everyone enough free will to express themselves through godly or ungodly works.

This truth means every man and woman alive are tested with trials and tribulations, as the humble Job was tested. For this reason, I call this habitation place where we live test ground Earth, and here on this Earth, Lucifer will test and try every one of us.

Therefore, I want you to realize that his attacks against us are attacks against our character. Because our character illustrates godliness or ungodliness, Lucifer will cast stumbling blocks in our pathway to prevent a righteous walk. Undoubtedly, trials and tribulations will reveal the quality of our character.

Furthermore, our personal God is identified by the voice we listen to and obey throughout our lifetime until we die. The voice of our all-mighty God comes from two different directions; one is His invisible Spirit, and the other is His righteous word.

Obviously, and as much as I wish it weren't true, this life we live in the flesh will not be a bed of roses on this Earth, and this is an obvious analogy involving everyone as we journey through this life, doing good and making mistakes we can absolve through repentance and change.

Life on this Earth can be much better for all of us if we're obedient to His word and conform to His righteous commandments, and thanks to God, He designed the right way to live. Furthermore, I am certain the rules of God are for everyone, and the residents in Heaven are living by the same design He designed for us.

The only difference is clear: Heaven's residents live by His commanded design and love it. However, no divine blessings are given to wicked and corrupt people who choose to live in opposition to Him. Sadly, the residents of this Earth aren't fighting temptations so well.

Furthermore, Christians do not have an exemption clause, and no divine blessings are given to a Christian for disobedience to His perfectly designed word. For this reason live a godly lifestyle and realize everything the God of Heaven and Earth says and does revolves around His beautiful Ten Commandments, His perfect design.

However, we all know that wicked people and disobedient Christians can work and labor for the blessing of prosperity. But the self-made blessing of prosperity hasn't any connection with divine healings and miracles from above.

However, all obedient Christians who are determined to keep His great Commandments and submit their will to His will are favored by Him. God will bless them in various ways other than prosperity and probably with a certain amount of prosperity.

Conclusively, Bible scriptures reveal the Good Shepherd hears the voice of His sheep in their times of trouble and needs. But I want you to know we must be obedient sheep and live by His required word. However, regardless of troubles and needs, we should obey His word.

Furthermore, I believe supernatural miracles occur on His extremely special, supernatural seventh-day Sabbath Day, mainly because the seventh day, Sabbath Day, was specially chosen by Him six thousand years ago. Indeed, for personal reasons, the seventh day rest day, is one of His designed commandments.

If we trade His special Sabbath Day for a counterfeit day, I guarantee we are saying God made a mistake when He wrote the fourth commandment. Sadly, recognizing the counterfeit Sabbath means we are saying keeping His special Sabbath Day isn't important.

Indeed, keeping the seventh day, Sabbath Day, defines believing men and women as obedient Christians, and obedient Christians are determined to honor Him with remembrance and thankfulness. But opposing the seventh day, Sabbath Day defines compromisers or covenant breakers.

Therefore, regardless of what promises or favors, many Christians believe to be free from God. It may not be free without being earned one way or another. This truth means supernatural and divine miracles, healings, and prosperity aren't given away by God like free popcorn at the movies.

Indeed, I want you to know supernatural miracles, healings, and prosperity earned arduously are a sign, and the sign means Christians are doing the will of God. Indeed, whenever we do the will of God, His heart is touched, and mercy is given from above.

Although, since we are none good in the flesh, and perfection is similar to reaching for the stars high in the sky, we cannot reach. It doesn't change the word of God, nor does it mean we can relax and forget about trying to be perfect in His ways.

This truth means regardless of our mistakes, we are still required to try and be Christ-like in our walk and talk and the works we do before the eyes of God. God will certainly respect all Christians, determined to obey and honor Him on His seventh-day Sabbath Day.

Furthermore, during the seventh day of the week, God always expects the same thing from believers in Him, regardless of their generation. Truly, it would be wise for us to realize we need to settle down on the seventh day and devote our time to learning about Him.

The seventh day is His hallowed, holy, sacred, and set apart day, and I want you to know that much devotion is missing from any Christian who accepts a counterfeit Sabbath Day. Sadly, I shouldn't have to tell you the simple truth, but keeping a counterfeit Sabbath Day instead of His authentic Sabbath Day is similar to having a black spot on a white robe.

Positively, the special God-created seventh day, Sabbath Day, has a significant meaning to God, and keeping it inspires Him to respond to personal prayer requests. We would be foolish to believe trading His authentic Sabbath Day for a counterfeit Sabbath Day is okay with Him.

Keeping the seventh holy day, Sabbath Day opens the windows of Heaven, and it doesn't have limitations, such as the counterfeit first day of the week, Sun-day, which is bound in chains by the commandments. I assure you that making the word of God of no effect is a strong limitation concerning divine blessings.

Indeed, the counterfeit Sun-day Sabbath Day was given to Christians under distress and through brutal force. But regardless of the way it was introduced into the Sun-day churches, it's still a manmade counterfeit Sabbath Day. Furthermore, the traditions of men and everything else contrary to God's word are counterfeit.

Beyond the shadow of a doubt, the counterfeit Sun-day Sabbath Day probably is the biggest lie in the Sun-day Churches today. Sadly, the devil deceives many people, and most preachers, teachers, and the congregation aren't aware of their conformity to the big lie.

This truth means whenever a Sun-day Christian chooses to keep the Sabbath on Sun-day, the first day of the week. Then, Bible scriptures reveal they do the opposite of our Great Creator God's commands, and we break the covenant with Him every time we oppose His commands.

Positively, I want you to know no flesh and blood man has the authority to change His sacred fourth commandment or any of His commandments. Undoubtedly, if we change a commandment of God, we please the wicked Lucifer, a rebellious counterfeit god.

I assure you that correctness comes from the perfect word of God, and incorrectness comes from the traditions of men. This truth means shaking hands on Sun-day mornings and singing about what it's like up there will not change or relax the authentic word of God or draw us closer to Him.

Many scriptures reveal the truth throughout our great Bible, including the fourth commandment. His commandments will tell us what's correct and authentic for our benefit, and I will tell you great wisdom: if we fear or respect the Lord, we shouldn't break His commandments.

Indeed, the fourth commandment is one of the most direct, to-the-point, and important statements explaining correctness. For our benefit, it's written clearly and has easy-to-understand commands from our creator God.

The fourth commandment is written so the simplest minds cannot misinterpret it. Because it's easy to understand, there's no room for anyone to assume the wrong definition of the fourth commandment because of its perfect clarity.

The extremely important and unchangeable fourth commandment tells us the hallowed Sabbath Day of the Lord is on the seventh day. Our wonderful Creator God makes this statement, and it couldn't be said any clearer, and He didn't tell us we substitute it for another day.

Truly, the authenticity of the fourth commandment shouldn't be surprising news to a Sun-day Christian if they love digging for the truth. Mainly because the seventh day, Sabbath Day, isn't hidden from their eyes if they search the scriptures for the truth of God.

However, if you find yourself living outside the truth and do not enjoy living outside the truth, then you should know the righteous word of God is a two-edged sword. Its truth is unchangeable, and His gospel shows no difference between people anywhere on the Earth.

I assure you, the sword of the Lord cuts anyone who falls under its blade of truth, and keeping the Sun-day Sabbath Day and calling it the Lord's Day has consequences attached to whoever makes the unauthorized Sabbath Day trade.

Conclusively, divine blessings and miracles are a reward for knowing and doing the authentic word of God. But self-made blessings are usually blessings of prosperity, and a time will arise in all our lives when we'll need more from God than prosperity.

Anyway, blessings of prosperity are usually the only blessings most men seek after, while they are strong and healthy. Truly, blessings of prosperity make us all feel good and secure until the rains come, and it rains upon us too much.

Positively, please be aware blessings of prosperity will not help us in any way win the prize of immortality. This truth means intangible divine blessings from God are worth much more than tangible self-made blessings.

The above statement is a fact most people will not realize until they are lying on their deathbed or standing before the judgment throne of God. But every person alive will wish they were Bible-savvy and full of understanding at the end of their life.

Mainly because we'll all be proud to stand before God and say, I loved your word so much; I studied it every chance I got. But the truth is clear, and observation proves nearly everyone living in this world is in trouble with God.

Furthermore, I am certain most people in this world will not be able to stand before our Great Creator God and truthfully say they loved His word and studied it regularly. But I hope and pray that you'll study His word daily and not stand before His Judgment Throne Bible illiterate.

CHAPTER THIRTY-SIX

MORTAL AND IMMORTAL

This informative story, Mortal and Immortal, illustrates a character divide among the creations of our Great Creator God. I want you to realize this divide is by the design of God, and it'll take a personal transition to overcome the divide and be one of the immortals.

This story also illustrates what we are now and can be in the future, which means our current lifestyle challenges the gift of immortality. Especially if we aren't serious about becoming a new Christ-like person and aren't hot and on fire for the perfect word of God.

Furthermore, we flesh and blood people living on this Earth are mortals, and being made from the dirt of this Earth means our transition period is still being considered from the Heavens above. Make cautious decisions and realize every day we live and breathe adds or takes away to our transition.

Positively, all the saints gone before us are the immortals because they've prevailed against the wicked Lucifer and won the prize of immortality. The saints are our role models, and for the privilege to be immortal, we'll have to accomplish the accomplishments they've made, too.

Conclusively, equal opportunity means generation after generation passes by, and every person therein, each generation, is offered the opportunity to win the prize of immortality. We should take our opportunity seriously, but winning the grand prize will require a few things from us.

Truly, I fully believe out of each generation, some loyal men and women win the prize of immortality because they love righteousness and have gladly conformed to God's perfect word. I want you to know that conforming to His word is the road map to eternity, but we will have to focus on the road map.

Sadly, to say, many people will lose their battle with the devil, and they'll not win the wonderful prize of immortality. It'll be because they refuse to conform to the perfect word of God, and I conclude that Lucifer's power of telepathy keeps men and women from conforming to His word.

I want you to know our battle against the wicked Lucifer and his powerful influence is real. Indeed, our testing on this Earth is real, and Heaven and Hell are real, and we better consider our fight for eternal life as real. In your daily walk, I want you to remember that demonic spirits are always prodding you and me to sin.

Indeed, after the death of our flesh, the testing on the Earth is over, and win or lose, it is report card time. I want to remind you being lukewarm or cold on the Judgment Scales of God illustrates the same thing as getting an "F" on our report card.

After we die in the flesh and our character is judged, we will receive the gift of immortality or lose immortality. This truth means the way we live our lifestyle is a barometer, and the barometer indicates immortality, or damnation, in the next lifetime.

Surely, suppose men and women weren't so spiritually blind and so concerned about the cares of this world. In that case, they might give more thought to the gift of immortality and the penalty of damnation and be more serious concerning all their decisions.

I assure you, thinking about the next life daily as we live and breathe on this Earth is important, mainly because not thinking about the next life will leave us unprepared on Judgment Day. Therefore, I warn you, put away foolishness and present yourselves before the Mediator as a loyal believer in Christ.

Truly, anyone with a brain in their head should understand immortality is much better than the judgment of damnation. But we must believe in God before we can believe in the reality of immortality and the terrible judgment of damnation.

I assure you the perfect word of God defines everything, and men guilty of refusing to believe in God are identified as the spiritually blind. The definition means Spiritual blindness is caused by unbelief, and immortality is beyond the unbeliever's reach.

However, even though they are flesh and blood, men and women are mortals made from the dirt of this Earth, have a short lifespan, and are compared to a vapor, here and gone. But the death of the flesh and blood body doesn't necessarily mean death to our spirit.

Positively, our spirit isn't made from the substance of dirt, and it'll not go back to the dirt of the Earth the way the flesh on our bones will. Truly, our inner spirit, given to us from the heavens above, is the only part of us, not made of dirt or flesh. But it originates from the Ancient of Days, the temple of God, and the Living Coals of Fire.

Therefore, each man, woman, and child living on this Earth possesses something immortal. Compliments of our Great God, our spirit is much older than our flesh and blood body and much more meaningful than the substance of our formation.

Furthermore, our gift is a small portion of the living God element, making every flesh and blood dirt man alive. The small piece of immortality all men possess is the spirit, and the spirit can make dirt bodies animated and alive.

The spirit within us is called by different names, just as many Bible characters have different names, but the spirit doesn't die because the flesh dies. But the death of the flesh releases our spirit, and our spirit moves forward to the next phase of life.

The conclusive end of life for the flesh and blood man reveals the dirt returning to the dirt. But our spirit journeys onward into a destiny determined by the lifestyle we've lived in the flesh. I want you to realize our new destiny will win us a new Christ-like body if we've given our loyalty to God.

Conclusively, it's wrong to believe dirt bodies have any immortality. Nor do dirt bodies exist in Hell, where the ungodly are imprisoned within the center of this Earth, simply because our dirt bodies do not exist in Hell or have a prophesized future.

I am certain because the next scripture says so when it says dirt returns to the Earth, as it was in the beginning. The great preacher man tells us that dust returns to dust, and the spirit returns to our Great Creator God.

Ecclesiastes 12:7 Then shall the <u>dust</u> (means the dirt body) return to the Earth as it was:

It may seem unfair for the mortal dirt man to see the vulnerability and the frailty of their flesh and blood life. But the fact remains clear: dust returns to dust sooner or later, and we all know death is unavoidable.

Ecclesiastes 12:7 And the <u>spirit</u> (the spark of life, the essence of pure energy, or the God element) shall return unto God who <u>gave</u> <u>it</u> (the spirit to the host dirt body, which God made flesh and blood animated and alive).

Surely, the above scripture reveals our wonderful Creator God is the giver of life, and it's His Spirit, allowing dirt to walk and talk. This truth means the Spirit of Life, the Spark of Life, and the Living Coals of Fire belong to Him.

Furthermore, when animated dirt returns to plain dirt, the living Spirit of God returns to God, and it would be naïve to believe our spirit dies with the flesh. However, for various ungodly reasons, the God of Heaven and Earth puts unthankful spirits in a different habitation place.

Positively, two different habitation places mean the example of the good and the bad being mixed on this Earth, changing after our flesh's death, and the change is good for believers in Christ, but it's bad for the unbelievers.

This truth means every person's spirits are divided; they'll never be mixed again, and compatibility will dwell with compatibility forever. The tares will live with the tares, and the loyal believers in Christ will live with Christ, which is the dream the believers dream.

However, just as the ugly caterpillar changes, it will look and transform into a beautiful butterfly, as does the mortal man put on beautiful immortality if he believes in Jesus Christ and claims Him as his Savior from eternal death. I want to tell you the Son of God is the only mediator between you and me and God.

Positively, the mortals become immortals after the death of the flesh if they've adhered to the conclusion to the whole matter. I want you to know the conclusion to the whole matter reveals the formula for obtaining the gift of immortality.

The next three revealing scriptures are the words of the Apostle Paul, and he makes it clear the kingdom of God doesn't have flesh and blood residents. The next three revealing scriptures suggest immortality happens after the death of our flesh if we are believers in God.

1 Corinthians 15:50 Now <u>I</u> (the Apostle Paul) say, <u>brethren</u> (believers in Christ), that flesh and blood cannot inherit the kingdom of God; neither doth corruption put on incorruption.

Indeed, before I give you these next three scriptures, it's important to realize that the Apostle Paul is speaking to believing brethren in Christ. When he uses the word incorruptible, he's talking about everyone determined to believe in following the examples of Christ.

The incorruptible in the kingdom of God are His children, who before us lived on this Earth and put the perfect word of God first every day of their lives. The incorruptible is a changed body, not flesh and blood anymore.

Positively, when he uses the word corruptible, he says corruption cannot be a part of the body of the incorruptible. Then he's saying the corruptible has a different destination after the death of the flesh. Thanks to God, the incorruptible will be separated from the corruptible someday.

However, the Apostle Paul analogy has a dual meaning: even the flesh made from dirt is corruptible, and maybe pureness of the heart is unachievable for the flesh man, and he cannot become incorruptible until we put on immortality and enter into a new Christ-like body.

1 Corinthians 15:52 In a moment, in the twinkling of an eye, at the last trump: For the trumpet shall sound, and the dead shall be raised incorruptible, and we shall be changed.

1 Corinthians 15:53 For this <u>corruptible</u> (flesh and blood dirt body) must put on **<u>incorruption</u>** (means inherit a heavenly body for the spirit departed from the flesh at death).

1 Corinthians 15:53 And the mortal must put on immortality.

I am certain the Apostle Paul is talking about the same spirit that departs from our flesh body and goes back to our Great Creator God every time a person in Christ dies. This truth means it'll be the same spirit we shared life with while being alive in the flesh, putting on immortality.

This truth means that if it's our spirit, we'll be the incorruptible residents in His special kingdom. Finally, after trials and tribulations, and after the death of the flesh, and after the knowledge of God, and the examples of the angels.

Including the examples of the immortal Most High God, the immortal Son of God, and the immortal Earth, the approved man or woman of God will know how it feels to be immortal and have the strength and health we cannot imagine.

Therefore, I am quite certain the message the great preacher is trying to tell us we should already know. Surely, he's saying life is too short to live a corrupt lifestyle, die ungodly, and miss out on the great gift of immortality.

Furthermore, the corruption of the heart is the characteristic that separates the humble and godly man from the vain and ungodly man. We all should realize there's no absolute promise of tomorrow for the flesh and blood person, and right now is the time to amend our flaws and conform to godliness.

However, living an ungodly lifestyle sends the spirit down instead of up, and corruption doesn't put on incorruption from the pits of Hell. Surely, if our spirit descends into the abyss of the Earth, becoming incorruptible will be impossible to achieve.

Therefore, while there's still time left to make lifestyle choices and live for God, please realize there is no promise of eternal longevity to the mortal dirt body. Truly, by our Great Creator God's design, the dirt body will deteriorate in time, and we better not waste our lives away.

This truth means that unless we accept the wonderful Son of God as our Savior, our absolute promise to live forever is being cast into the lake of fire. The Lake of Fire is specially made for wicked and rebellious unbelievers.

I am certain the Lake of Fire residents will not have a divine Savior, and throwing them a rescue device isn't prophesized anywhere in the Bible. For this reason, we better find our Savior and love Him before it's too late.

Positively, you, I, and everyone else should realize life is as fragile as glass, and it only endures for a little while. But before the glass breaks, the treasures of our hearts will be revealed in this short amount of time. Also, in this short amount of time, the degree of love we have for God will be revealed.

For this reason, I warn you that too many Earthly endeavors for material wealth and gain point to vexation and vanity, and the flesh will not profit anything from economic works after the death of the flesh.

This truth means it is vanity and vexation to seek Earthly treasures, not seek after God's commanded ways with the same vigor and enthusiasm. Indeed, the definition of foolish entwines with whoever is wasting their life away.

It's for this reason, and because I also care about where your soul goes I want you to know for certain an unchallengeable truth. The only things of real tangible profit in this life, identified as non-corruptible, are God's pure at-heart works.

Indeed, the works of the flesh will pass away, but the excellent works of God are here to stay. Thanks to the mercy of God, we can be a part of His plan and dream and have a glorious salvation day if we stay steadfast in His wonderful and infallible word.

1 Corinthians 15:58 Therefore, my beloved brethren, be ye steadfast, unmovable, always abounding in the work of the Lord, for as much as ye know that your labor is not in vain in the Lord.

Mainly because of creation and the wonderful and perfect word of God, and the examples of His Son, who came down to this Earth as a mortal man, humble as a lamb, the good works of God can be seen throughout every generation, and every day through men determined to carry the gospel of God, wherever their footsteps go in this world.

The wonderful gospel of God assures us that man can win the prize of immortality, have a new incorruptible body, and live forever if our Creator God and the word of God mean more to us than the ungodly things of this world.

Therefore, my advice to every person on this Earth is serious and meaningful. I am telling you, we better pick up the wonderful cross of Yeshua and proudly carry it every day of our lives before the eyes of all men.

However, I warn you, do not be ashamed of the wonderful gospel of God, lest Christ be ashamed of you when you stand before Him on Judgment Day. Undoubtedly, the course of mankind was planned by the Ancient of Days, and someday soon, it'll be our turn to meet Him face to face.